The Morality of Terrorism

Conflict and Consciousness
Studies in War, Peace, and Social Thought

Charles Webel
General Editor

Vol. 4

PETER LANG
New York • Washington, D.C./Baltimore • Boston
Bern • Frankfurt am Main • Berlin • Vienna • Paris

Haig Khatchadourian

The Morality of Terrorism

PETER LANG
New York • Washington, D.C./Baltimore • Boston
Bern • Frankfurt am Main • Berlin • Vienna • Paris

Library of Congress Cataloging-in-Publication Data

Khatchadourian, Haig.
The morality of terrorism / Haig Khatchadourian.
p. cm. — (Conflict and consciousness; 4)
Includes bibliographical references and index.
1. Terrorism—Moral and ethical aspects. I. Title. II. Series:
Conflict and consciousness; vol. 4.
HV6431.K43 179.7—dc21 97-8540
ISBN 0-8204-3790-5
ISSN 0899-9910

Die Deutsche Bibliothek-CIP-Einheitsaufnahme

Khatchadourian, Haig:
The morality of terrorism / Haig Khatchadourian.
–New York; Washington, D.C./Baltimore; Boston; Bern;
Frankfurt am Main; Berlin; Vienna; Paris: Lang.
(Conflict and consciousness; 4)
ISBN 0-8204-3790-5 Gb.

Cover design by James F. Brisson.

The paper in this book meets the guidelines for permanence and durability
of the Committee on Production Guidelines for Book Longevity
of the Council of Library Resources.

© 1998 Peter Lang Publishing, Inc., New York

Printed in the United States of America.

To my wife Arpiné

Acknowledgments

I wish to thank the following for permission to reprint parts or the whole of some of my previously published articles:

The Edwin Mellen Press for parts of Criteria Of Territorial Rights Of Peoples and Nations, which appeared in *The Territorial Rights Of Nations and Peoples, Studies in World Peace*, Volume 2, edited by John R. Jacobson, 1989.

Journal of Applied Philosophy, edited by Brenda Almond, for Morality and Terrorism, October 1988.

Mercat Press for Just Revolution, which appeared in *Shaping Revolution*, edited by Elspeth Attwooll, Aberdeen University Press, 1991.

Contents

Introduction

There exists a good deal of confusion and misunderstanding, as well as deliberate distortion, disinformation, and propaganda, about the nature of terrorism and so-called freedom fighting. Terrorism and "freedom fighting" are continually used as political weapons by parties locked in violent conflict, but discussions of the nature of these weapons often leave much to be desired. In fact, perhaps because of the widespread, unquestioning assumption that terrorism is always wrong, moral philosophers have paid too little attention to the question of the morality of terrorism, although the situation appears to be gradually changing. The situation is not much better with regard to the morality of "counterterrorism" or of "freedom fighting," a euphemism for revolutionary liberationist civil wars, uprisings, rebellions and revolutions, coups d'etat, and guerilla warfare.

The initial aim of this book is therefore to try to provide, in Chapters 1 and 5, a more adequate analytical account or understanding of the concepts of terrorism and "freedom fighting," and to distinguish them from each other.

The second aim is to provide a reasoned evaluation of the morality of terrorism, which appears mainly in Chapters 2 and 4 and in the appendix to Chapter 4, and of the morality of "freedom fighting," in Chapter 5; and to draw attention to the moral pitfalls and possible misuses of judicial, "antiterrorist" responses to terrorism and to certain highly unethical measures and strategies of state "counterterrorism," in Chapter 6. Chapter 3 attempts to provide a rationale for the principles and rules of "just war" theory deployed in the evaluation of the morality of terrorism, "freedom fighting," and various antiterrorist/counterterrorist methods and strategies. No attempt is made to provide a rationale for the consequentialist moral considerations also deployed to evaluate them. To do so would require a separate treatise and would, in any case, carry the discussion too far afield. On the other hand, the human-rights principles also appealed to-particularly the foundational norm that all human beings have a human right to be treated as moral persons-are drawn from previously published material.

Chapter 7 ties the preceding chapters together, rounding off the discussion.

This book provides a general theoretical, philosophical-ethical consideration of certain types and forms of force and violence. But such an inquiry needs to be followed or complemented by some concrete, practical examples. More specifically, an analytic and normative consideration of terrorism and "freedom fighting" would be grossly incomplete if it does not additionally provide a fairly detailed case study of at least one major contemporary example of sustained political, or moralistic/religious terrorist activity, or of terorist activity together with "freedom fighting." Such a case study would include an account of (a) the deep-lying or historical-cultural root causes of some particular political or moralistic/religious terrorist activity or of terrorist activity together with "freedom fighting"; hence (b) its motivation; and (c) the goals, particularly the long-range or ultimate goals, of the terrorists or the "freedom fighters."

Palestinian and other Arab terrorism is the prime example of contemporary international political-moralistic/religious terrorism, and has sometimes included not only terrorism by members of a particular country targeting their own government or some foreign government or governments (terrorism from below), but also, in the case of some Middle Eastern countries, state- or state-sponsored terrorism (terrorism from above). The destructive effects of that terrorism have also been felt beyond the Middle East, in Europe and the United States, and therefore more widely than other contemporary examples of terrorist violence. In addition, the two other forms of the Arabs' armed struggle against Israel—the series of wars as well as the Palestinian "freedom fighting," which included the Palestinian intifada–had the same historical root cause as the terrorism, and were waged with the same or similar ultimate goals.

With these things in mind, the Appendix outlines the historical root cause of the Arab-Israeli conflict in general and the Palestinian-Israeli conflict in particular, namely, the Palestine Problem, including a brief account of the moral and legal territorial rights of Palestinians and Jews.

An important reason for my emphasis, in this Introduction and in the Appendix, on a proper understanding of root causes of political and moralistic/religious terrorism and other forms of violence considered in this book, is that these and many other forms of violence cannot be prevented or eliminated without peacefully addressing those deep-lying root causes. In the case of political-moralistic/religious terrorism, for instance, no amount of antiterrorism or (even) counterterrorism, however stringent or rigorously applied, can come close to eradicating it. They can only address the symptoms, not the underlying cause(s). Only by the elimination of the terrorism's root-causes can the world hope to succeed in greatly reducing if not putting an end to it.

The peaceful elimination of the historical root cause of Palestinian and other Arab terrorism, essentially means the peaceful resolution of the Palestine Problem together with the other, more recent causes of Syria's and Lebanon's territorial and other disputes with Israel.

The Appendix tries to be as fair and objective as possible to the various sides in the Arab-Israeli conflict, by drawing, as much as space permits, on the work of professional historians and scholars: Arab, Israeli, British, and American. But objectivity in such emotionally-charged matters cannot but be a matter of degree, especially in the interpretation of the crucial historical facts and in the moral evaluation of the different roles played by the major protagonists. In the evaluation of terrorism, "freedom fighting," and responses to terrorism in the body of the book, I have attempted to be fair to major contemporary ethical approaches in moral philosophy, by appealing to both deontological and consequentialist principles in the form of human rights, "just war" theory, and consequentialism, including act-/and rule-utilitarianism. In that way my approach has been broader than it would have been had appeal been made to some particular contemporary deontological or consequentialist theory. However, no appeal has been made to contemporary feminist ethic of care, to the extent that it can comfortably apply to terrorism, "freedom fighting," etc., although doing so might have been quite illuminating with regard to its reach and its limits as an ethic. Nor is an appeal made to any "postmodern" ethical theory or approach, of which I must presently plead ignorance.

It is important to note that the book is about both violence and nonviolence, about the deterring and prevention of terrorism, counterterrorism, and "freedom fighting." More positively, it is about the quest for stability, justice, and peace in our world. Indeed, given the great evil of violence, the quest for peace, justice, and stability is by far its more fundamental subject and aim.

At the end of one of the bloodiest centuries in the history of humankind, we sorely need to seek nonviolent alternatives to violence, including terrorism, both old and new. Short of a revolutionary improvement in human nature, which may or may not ever come about, the avoidance of serious conflict requires a much better empathic understanding of the aspirations and concerns of others, of their values and way of life, as well as a respect for them as persons. This is especially true in relation to peoples who belong to a very different civilization, where the danger of objectifying them is greatest. Only then would real toleration and acceptance of differences become a reality.

With regard to the international political and military domains, it is my firm belief that the United States, in tandem with the United Nations, ought to try to play, as much as possible, a leading role in possibly averting and in resolving serious political/military tensions in parts of the world with the potential for revolution, war, or genocide. It is also necessary, I believe, that the United Nations mandate be broadened to permit it, under carefully laid down conditions, to use its powers to try to make peace where peace is most threatened. For that purpose, as well as for peacekeeping, the creation of a special standing United Nations' military force would be highly desirable.

Apart from overpopulation, the greatest threat to humankind is the danger of nuclear war. The world will never be safe from nuclear holocaust unless and until all nuclear weapons are destroyed and no such weapons are ever produced again. But it is unlikely in the extreme that the present nuclear powers, particularly the United States, Russia, and China would even imagine doing so (although even at this moment some former American and Russian generals are urging the nuclear powers to do so). A rational and moral alternative would be for them to place their nuclear arsenals under the jurisdiction of the United Nations, which would then create a special task force to oversee the gradual but eventual complete destruction of these weapons, using for that purpose special funds from the world community.

One of the more encouraging practical alternatives to violence, in this case war, has been the creation of the European Union with its promise of increasing unity and lasting peace among its members in the coming years and decades. It is my hope that that union will become an inspiration and a model for countries in other parts of the world, transcending old animosities and hatreds, paving the way for cooperative and long-lasting peaceful existence.

I mentioned the importance of empathy in efforts to understand others, particularly those who differ culturally. There is perhaps no better way to do so than to experience the others' way of life firsthand by living among them-provided we are genuinely open and receptive to their aspirations and concerns. That is precisely the source of my own personal and intellectual interest in the subjects treated in this book; namely, my Middle Eastern heritage as an Armenian and former Palestinian, born and bred in the Holy Land. That fact has enabled me, I believe, to see more clearly the conflicting Arab and Israeli points of view, and to identify existentially with the hopes, aspirations, and sufferings of both Arabs and Jews locked in a tragic conflict.

Chapter 1

What Terrorism Is And Is Not

Terrorism: What's in a Name?

What terrorism is or how the word should be employed is a much vexed question, and many definitions of it have been proposed. Some of the conceptual reasons for the lack of agreement on its meaning will become clearer as I proceed, but the fact that the term is almost invariably used in an evaluative—indeed, highly polemical and emotionally charged—way makes the framing of a neutral definition a difficult task. It is probably no exaggeration to say that, at present, it is as emotional a word as "war." In fact, some think of terrorism as a kind of war, and the mere mention of the word arouses similar anxieties and fears. This was particularly true at the time the initial draft of this chapter was being written, against the backdrop of the Gulf War and President Saddam Hussein's repeated warnings of terrorism against American and European interests world-wide. Not surprisingly, therefore, terrorism is very widely condemned as a major evil plaguing the last decades of the Twentieth century, a century already drenched with the blood of the innocent and the noninnocent in a long series of wars, revolutions, civil wars, and other forms of violence.

The widespread condemnation of terrorism as an unmitigated evil stems in part from the fact that some of those governments or countries, political systems, or regimes, that are the main targets, particularly of state or state-sponsored political violence, use the word as a political-psychological weapon in their fight against the perpetrators and their avowed causes—for example, national liberation from foreign occupation or the overthrow of an oppressive indigenous system or regime. In fighting terrorism targeted at them, the victim groups or countries tend to indiscriminately label all their enemies as "terrorists," including those who practice the least violent kinds of protest, thus stretching the word's already loose usage and vague meaning beyond reason.[1] Despite its notorious vagueness and looseness, some overlap among the multiplicity of the word's definitions and characterizations exists. Quite a number of definitions in the literature, as well as characterizations in the media and in everyday discourse, include the idea that terrorism is the threat or the actual use of violence—the unlawful use of force—[2] directed against civilians (e.g. noncombatants in wartime) *and they alone*, sometimes with the addition of the words, "*for political* purposes." In that respect the moral philosopher Douglas Lackey's definition is typical. With wartime terrorism in mind, he writes: "What separates the terrorist from the traditional revolutionary is a persistent refusal to direct violence at military objectives. Terrorism, on this account, is the threat or use of violence against noncombatants for political purposes. In ordinary war, the deaths of civilians are side effects of military operations directed against military targets. In terrorist operations, the civilian is the direct and intentional target of attack."[3] The same putative core of meaning occurs in other definitions I shall consider.

Although I shall argue that this and similar definitions of "terrorism" are inadequate, Lackey is right in rejecting the definition of former Vice-President George Bush's Task Force on Combating Terrorism, according to which terrorism is "the unlawful use or threat of violence against persons or property to further political or social objectives."[4] That definition, Lackey notes, is too broad, but his own definition suffers from the opposite defect, although it has the merit of not confining the victims of terrorism to civilians. Another example of a too-broad definition is the Task Force's "the threatened or actual use of force or violence to attain a political goal through fear, coercion, or intimidation."[5]

The preceding and most of the other definitions that have been proposed share a more fundamental defect, one that will be noted as we proceed.

Other proposed definitions I have examined[6] are also either too broad or too narrow, or both-a problem faced by "essentialist" definitions in general-often in addition to other defects. Some definitions are too restrictive, being limited to one form of terrorism, for example, political terrorism in the usual, restricted meaning of the word.[7] Still other definitions or characterizations fail because they are overtly or covertly normative (condemnatory) rather than, as definitions ought to be, neutral or nonevaluative. Former President Ronald Reagan's statement that terrorism is the deliberate maiming or killing of innocent people, and his characterization of terrorists as "base criminals," clearly beg the ethical issues.[8] A fuller definition that suffers from the same flaw among others, is proposed by Burton Leiser. Part of his definition is:[9]

> *Terrorism* is any organized set of acts of violence designed to destroy the structure of authority which normally stands for security, or to reinforce and perpetuate a governmental regime whose popular support is shaky. It is a policy of seemingly senseless, irrational, and arbitrary murder, assassination, sabotage, subversion, robbery and other forms of violence, all committed with dedicated indifference to existing legal and moral codes or with claims to special exemption from conventional social norms.

Elements of Terrorism

The main forms of terrorism in existence in the present-day world share at least five important aspects or elements which an adequate description of terrorism must include. They are:

1. The historical and cultural, including the socioeconomic root causes of its prevalence (e.g., the lack or loss of a homeland).
2. The immediate, intermediate and long-range or ultimate goals. Retaliation is an example of the first, while publicity is an example of the second. The regaining of a lost homeland, the acquisition or exercise of power [by a state], . . . or enforcement of [its] authority",[10] (which F. J. Hacker calls terrorism from above[11]), or the challenge to . . . [a state's] authority (which he calls terrorism from below) are examples of long range terrorist goal.
3. The third aspect or element consists in the forms and methods of coercion and force[12] generally resorted to to

terrorize the immediate victims and to coerce[13] those who
are seriously affected by the terrorism, the victimized.
The latter are the individuals, groups, governments, or
countries that are intimately connected with the immediate targets and who are themselves the real albeit indirect targets of the terrorist acts.[14] The forms and methods of coercion and force resorted to define the different
species or *forms* of terrorism of any given *type*.

4. The nature or kinds of organizations and institutions, or
   the political systems, practicing or sponsoring the terrorism. For example, in state terrorism the terrorism is
   practiced by agents of a state, while in state-sponsored
   terrorism the terrorism is financially, militarily, or in
   other ways supported but not directly conducted by the
   sponsoring state or states.

5. The social, political, economic or military context or circumstances in which the terrorism occurs is also important and must be considered. For example, whether the
   terrorism occurs in time of peace or in wartime.[15] In the
   latter case, there is also an important ethical dimension
   in relation to terrorist violence or threats to noncombatants, just as in the case of precision "saturation" bombing of towns and cities in Twentieth century warfare. This
   would become incalculably more important in the case
   of possible nuclear terrorism.[16]

The one form of terrorism to which (1) above does not normally apply is predatory terrorism—terrorism motivated by
greed. But predatory terrorism is relatively unimportant, especially for a discussion of the morality of terrorism such as
the present one, since it is clearly immoral. Although seriously
flawed, Leiser's definition noted earlier has the merit of in-
corporating several of the aspects of terrorism I have mentioned. But it fails to spell out the various sorts of causes of
terrorism and makes only a passing mention of what it calls
the terrorists' "political ends."[17]

Defining "Terrorism"

A fully adequate characterization or formal definition of "terrorism" must be as neutral as possible and not beg the issue of

the morality of terrorism in general, in addition to reflecting the five aspects or dimensions of terrrorism distinguished above-notwithstanding the word's almost invariably negative connotations, particularly in the Western world.

I stated earlier that Leiser's and certain other definitions of the word describe terrorism as *always* involving the maiming, killing, or coercion of innocent, and *only* innocent, persons, by which Leiser means "persons who have little or no direct connection with the causes to which the terrorists are dedicated."[18] Although this definition is not quite clear on the point, Leiser appears to equate terrorism with what he calls "the victimization of defenseless, innocent persons" as opposed to "the assassination of political and military leaders [political assassination]."[19]

In the current literature the question of whether noninnocents can be included among the immediate victims of terrorism appears to be a very unsettled question. The absence of clarity and fixity-indeed, the ambivalence and uncertainty in current employments of the word—reflect the different users' stand on the *morality* of terrorism and the morality, especially, of the unlawful use of force in general. These uncertainties are intimately connected with uncertainties concerning the distinction between terrorism and "freedom fighting," such as a rebellion, a civil war, an uprising, or a guerilla war aiming, for example, at national liberation. Those who consider the harming of innocent persons an essential feature of terrorism would tend to consider "freedom fighting" as involving, *inter alia*, the maiming, killing or coercing of *non*innocents. That would allow "political assassination" to be classified as a species of "freedom fighting." Leiser states that guerilla warfare is characterized by small-scale, unconventional, limited actions carried out by irregular forces *"against regular military forces, their supply lines, and communications."*[20] That description would be perfectly in order provided we stipulate that the targeted soldiers are in the army of their own free will.

The preceding discussion indicates that in addition to being open textured and vague, the various current evaluative concepts of terrorism, like all other evaluative concepts, are, in W.B. Gallie's phrase, "essentially contested."[21] Yet like most vague and unsettled expressions "terrorism" has a "common core of meaning" in its different usages. This core of meaning includes the notion that terrorist acts are acts of coercion or of actual use of force,[22] aiming at monetary gain (*predatory terrrorism*), revenge (*retaliatory terrorism*), a political end (*political terrorism*), or a putative moral/religious end (*moralistic/religious terrorism*).[23]

What is absolutely essential for an adequate concept of terrorism and helps distinguish it from all other uses of force or coercion, but which most definitions I have come across lack, is what I shall call terrorism's "bifocal" character. I mean the crucial distinction between (a) the "immediate victims," the individuals who are the immediate targets of terrorism, and (b) "the victimized," those who are the indirect but real targets of the terrorist acts. Normally the latter are individual governments or countries or certain groups of governments or countries, or specific institutions or groups within a given country. The ultimate targets may also be certain social, economic or political systems or regimes which the terrorists dislike and hope to change or destroy by their terrrorist activities.

Despite the importance and obviousness of the above distinction, very few general descriptions of terrorism other than Abraham Edel's appear to recognize it. One definition that does is Weinberg's and Davis's description of terrorism in their book, *Introduction to Political Terrorism*[9], although, unfortunately, their description of the terrorists' goals—"sending a message to some broader target population"—is vague and overly general. After some exploration of the merits of attempts to define the term connotatively or denotatively, they state: "The objective of harming immediate victims, e.g., passers by in a public square or vacation-bound passengers in a railroad station, is *subordinate* [indeed, only a means] *to the purpose of sending a message to some broader target population.*"[24]

Again, the frequent randomness and unpredictability of who will actually become "immediate victims" of seemingly irrational terrorist attacks is calculated to heighten the fear and anxiety of travelers at airports, bus, and railway stations, tourists on cruise boats, and customers in banks and other commercial institutions, particularly in countries continually targeted by terrorists.

As would be expected, the causes and the goals of terrorism differ with the different types of terrorism: predatory, retaliatory, and others. The methods used by the terrorists also vary depending on these and other factors.

Following the psychiatrist Frederick Hacker, Vetter et al. distinguish three kinds of terrorists:[25]

> *Crusaders, criminals, and crazies.* The crusader is one who seeks prestige and power in the service of a "higher cause" and acts to attain a collective goal. Criminals may commit acts of terrorism as individuals, such as the bank robber who tries to secure his getaway by seizing bank personnel or customers and holding them hostage, or as part of the pattern of intimidation and coercion practiced by syndicated (organized) crime. . . . Acts of terrorism . . . can be carried out by *crazies*, individuals who are mentally and emotionally disturbed.

Only the last form above is additional to the main forms of terrorism I have distinguished. Inasmuch as a psychotic terrorist acts out of unconscious forces, he or she cannot control or understand, and so *lacks* anything like a rational goal for which the acts of terrorism are putative means. Because of its relative rarity and very special nature I shall hereafter leave it aside. As regards *criminals*, they fall under "predatory terrorism," while the terrorism of crusaders, which "involves acts of *political violence*,"[26] falls under "political terrorism," and/or "moralistic/religious terrorism." Our categories of retaliatory, political, and/or moralistic/religious terrorism can also readily accomodate Thornton's "*agitational* terror[ism] (violence perpetrated by an organized group seeking to disrupt an existing political establishment and seize control), and *enforcement* terror[ism] (violence employed by governments to extinguish threats to their power and authority)."[27] Our three categories also accomodate the distinction between terrorism from above (e.g., Thornton's *enforcement* terrorism) and terrorism from below, which may be retaliatory, political, and/or moralistic/religious. Finally, the three forms of terrorism Weinberg and Davis distinguish—"national liberationist," "revolutionary," and "reactionary"—clearly fall under our political and/or moralistic/religious rubrics.

So-called state and state-sponsored terrorism, including nuclear state terrorism, are not (*pace* Edel) a distinct type or types of terrorism but a special form of political terrorism, and instances of state terrorism may also be, on occasion, instances of moralistic terrrorism. Political terrrorism, including state terrorism, is also often "international terrrorism" as defined by a resolution of the U.S. House of Representatives. The resolution includes a statement to the effect that an act of terror[28] is an act of international terror if it transcends the national boundaries of the perpetrators or is directed against foreign nationals within the perpetrators' national boundaries. The act also falls within the definition if it violates any of the provisions set under the *Convention for the Suppression of Unlawful Seizures of Aircraft*.[29]

Since many terrorist acts in history and during the last decades of the twentieth century have been politically motivated, a large part of the recent literature concentrates on political terrorism, and definitions of political terrorism abound. But as we have seen, some definitions that purport to define terrorism in general are in fact definitions of political terrorism alone. A particularly interesting example not mentioned earlier is the *legal definition* of the Federal Republic of Germany, which, Jonathan R. White writes,"has combated terrorism through the legal process. Terrorism [on that definition] is the use of criminal acts for *political purposes* or in such manner as to create political disorder, so West Germans have defined the crime of terrorism by law, and specific actions can be taken against terrorists who violate that law (Grosscup 1987), 215-240)."[30] I have italicized "political purposes" to emphasize the narrowness of this purported definition of "terrorism in general."

Paul Wilkinson, in addition to a careful discussion of the different characteristics of terrorism in general and of different varieties of terrorism,[31] makes an important, rarely-drawn distinction between terrorism and *terror*, and notes significant similarities between *terrorism* and *terror* as a technical or semitechnical term. He points out that the "various forms of psychic terror, whether self-induced or stimulated by art, religion, or indoctrination [e.g., the terror of Divine punishment or retribution]," are to be distinguished from terrorism, particularly political terrorism. The latter he defines as "the use of coercive intimidation by revolutionary movements, regimes or individuals for political motives."[32] Drawing on our own characterization of terrorism, it is seen that, as defined by Wilkinson, "terror" lacks, *inter alia*, the crucial "bifocality" of terrorism. On that criterion, the guillotining of rival revolutionaries whereby the French Revolution devoured its children, indeed comprised acts of terror. They were not (also) acts of terrorism, although the word "terrorism" reflects the fact that the terrorists' terrorizing of their immediate victims and the resultant coercion of those they victimize is crucial for their success. This fact is well captured in Raymond Aaron's remark that "An action of violence is labeled 'terrorist' when its psychological effects are out of proportion to its purely physical result."[33] Acts of terror too may (but need not) have that kind of effect. Whether particular terrorist acts succeed in doing so, they are always designed to inspire fear and even terror, in the ordinary meaning of the word, in those they target. But not all acts that inspire terror—whether in the ordinary or in Wilkinson's meaning of "terror"—in those they target, or in others, are acts of terrorism.

Wilkinson isolates several key characteristics of "terror": "indiscriminateness, unpredictability, arbitrariness, ruthless destructiveness and the implicitly amoral and antinomian nature of a terrorist's challenge."[34] Although "terror" can exist in the absence of terrorism, Wilkinson wrongly thinks that political terrorism always involves "terror." He says: "Political terrorism, properly speaking, is a sustained policy involving the waging of organized terror either on the part of the state, a movement or faction, or by a small group of individuals. Systematic terrorism invariably entails some organization structure, however rudimentary, and some kind of theory or ideology of terror."[35] I say "wrongly" because unlike "terror" as he himself characterizes it, political terrorism is almost invariably a sustained policy,[36] hence organized and systematic, not arbitrary. Admittedly, however, it shares some of the characteristics of "terror." It is ruthlessly destructive, unpredictable, and frequently indiscriminate with respect to its immediate victims, although not its real target, the victimized.[37]

Our discussion of some current uses of "terrrorism" bears out Edel's observation that terrorism "is an emerging concept rather than one endowed with an established essence, and what will emerge will be a quasitechnical usage on which will hang a variety of legal and moral consequences."[38] The definitions of "international terrorism" I noted reflect emerging quasitechnical legal uses, although they will probably be mainly concerned with political terrorism. (But recall the inadequate German legal definition noted earlier.)

In light of the complexity, diversity, and variability of the actions and activities currently covered by the term "terrorism," reflected in the five aspects of terrorism I distinguished, an *adequate essentialist* definition of what is now usually called terrorism appears to me to be impossible as well as undesirable. Rather, a "range definition" delimiting a certain kind of "family" concept would avoid the two opposite problems plaguing essentialist definitions or concepts in such cases: narrowness and overinclusiveness. Leiser's definition has the merit of characterizing terrorism in terms of a set of disjunctions reflecting the diversity of the goals and consequently the different types of terrorism. But since some broad features—determined by the word's common core of meaning—are shared by all acts of terrorism as the word is usually employed, *terrorism* is and may continue in future to be a "quasi-essentialist" concept. Such a concept is logically intermediate between an essentialist concept, defined in terms of a set of necessary and sufficient conditions, and a "pure family resemblance" concept,[39] solely and wholly and defined in terms of criss-crossing resemblances of different degrees of generality or specificity.

Political Assassination and Terrorism

One of the tools of retaliatory and political terrorism is the assassination or attempted assassination of political leaders for a political end; indeed, assassination may be calculated to produce fear, even panic, in a country or a people, sometimes as part of or as a prelude to a civil war, coup d'etat, or rebellion. Nevertheless, political assassination is logically distinct from terrorism. Like "terror" and other unlawful uses of force that differ from terrorism proper, it lacks the latter's essential bifocal character. When political assassination is used by terrorists it *ipso facto* acquires the hallmark of terrrorism, becomes bifocal in its purpose.

It follows that Weinberg and Davis are right in distinguishing terrorism and the assassination of political figures, but wrong in adding that the latter "may be undertaken for *terror-*

ist purposes, for example, when the person attacked has some broader symbolic meaning for a wider audience, but this need not always be the case. In many instances the object of attack is both victim and target."[40] Later they list assassination as one of the six tactics reputedly used in 95 percent of all contemporary terrorist incidents, the other 5 percent being bombings, kidnappings, barricade and hostage situations, and hijackings.[41]

To sum up, this chapter aims to dispel widespread confusions and correct misconceptions about the nature of terrorism, and to provide a more adequate, analytical understanding of it, including the classification of its main contemporary types and forms.

Examination of paradigm cases of terrorism shows that it is distinguished from all other kinds of violence by its "bifocal" character; namely, by the fact that the immediate acts of terrorist violence, such as shootings, bombings, kidnappings, and hostage-taking, are intended as means to certain goals. In the case of political or political-moralistic/religious terrorism in particular, the acts of violence are intended as means to certain intermediate or long-range or ultimate goals, which vary with the particular terrorist acts or series of such acts.

In its bifocal character, terrorism is distinguished from straightforward, monofocal acts of murder, sabotage, kidnapping, and hostage-taking as well as uprisings, rebellions, and revolutions, coups d'etat and civil war, and war. Consequently, as will be seen in Chapter 5, it is distinguished from those uprisings, rebellions, and so on that qualify as instances of "freedom fighting"—collective acts of force or violence aiming at freedom or liberation from domestic oppression or foreign rule.

Apart from its essential bifocal character, the concept of terrorism is a "family resemblance" concept, consisting of a "family" of types and forms related only by varying crisscrossing resemblances. Consequently, the concept as a whole is an "open" or "open-textured" concept, nonsharply demarcated from other types/forms of individual or collective violence. The major types of terrorism are: predatory, retaliatory, political, and political-moralistic/religious. The terrorism may be domestic or international, "from above"—i.e., state or state-sponsored terrorism—or "from below." Finally, terrorism may occur in time of peace or in time of war.

Notes

1. A notorious example, which carries this tendency to absurdity, is the late Mr. Rabin's calling the "stone children" of the Palestinian intifada "terrorists" in front of American television cameras. Mr. Rabin himself was murdered by a Jewish terrorist.

2. This is false in terrorism practiced by a ruling dictator or military junta, whenever the government's (or its military's) terrorist activities conform to (unjust) laws decreed by the dictator or junta.

3. Douglas Lackey, *The Ethics of War and Peace* (Englewood Cliffs, NJ, 1989), 85.

4. "Report of Vice-President's Task Force on Combating Terrorism," in Lackey, *Ethics*, 85.

5. Charles A. Russell et al., "Out-Inventing the Terrorist," in *Terrorism, Theory and Practice*, Yonah Alexander et al., eds. (Boulder, CO, 1979), 4. In note 2, p. 37, the authors add: "'Political' is understood in this usage to connote the entire range of social, economic, religious, ethnic, and governmental factors impacting on a body politic, stressing the notions of power and influence. The ideal definition is one that both the adherents and abhorrers of terrorism could agree upon."

6. According to Leonard B. Weinberg and Paul Davis, *Introduction to Political Terrorism* (New York, 1989), 3, more than one hundred separate definitions have been proposed by different analysts over the years. See also Harold J. Vetter et al., *Perspectives on Terrorism* (Pacific Grove, CA, 1990), 3, where it is stated that the definitions were formulated between 1936 and 1983.

7. For example, Weinberg and Davis' definition in their *Introduction*, 3ff.

8. Quoted in Haig Khatchadourian, "Terrorism and Morality," *Journal of Applied Philosophy*, 5, no. 2 (October 1988): 131.

9. Burton M. Leiser, *Liberty, Justice, and Morals* (New York, 1979), 375. Italics in original.

10. Vetter et al., *Perspectives*, 8.

11. Frederick J. Hacker, *Crusaders, Criminals, Crazies* (New York, 1977), quoted in Vetter et al., 8.

12. I use "force" because it is morally neutral or near-neutral, unlike the more common "violence."

13. Weinberg and Davis, Introduction, 6, state: "The objective purpose of harming immediate victims is subordinate to the purpose of send-

ing a messasge to some broader target population [the 'victimized'])."
Although this statement shows their recognition of the bifocal character of terrorism, the idea of "sending a message" is too general and
vague to be of much service.

14. I borrow "immediate victim" from Abraham Edel, "Notes on Terrorism," in *Values in Conflict*, Burton M. Leiser, ed. (New York, 1981),
458.

15. This and the next section are largely reproduced, with some stylistic
and substantive changes, from my "Terrorism and Morality."

16. Cf. Joel Kovel, *Against The State Of Nuclear Terror* (Boston, MA, 1983),
Robert J. Lifton and Richard Falk, *Indefensible Weapons* (New York,
1982), and Helen Caldicott, *Missile Envy, The Arms Race and Nuclear
War* (New York, 1986).

17. Leiser, *Liberty, Justice, and Morals*, 375.

18. Ibid.

19. Ibid., 379. Leiser's view of terrorism is crystallized in a section titled
"Terrorism: Enemies of Mankind," 389-391.

20. Ibid., 381. Italics in original.

21. W. B. Gallie, "Essentially Contested Concepts," *Proceedings of the Aris-
totelian Society*, n.s., 56 (March 1956), 180ff. But Gallie maintains that
a concept must have certain characteristics in addition to
appraisiveness (he enumerates them on pp. 171-172) to be "essentially contested" in his sense.

22. Those who use "terrorism" as a condemnatory term would substitute
"violence" for "force."

23. I borrow the categories "predatory" and "moralistic" from Edel, "Notes
on Terrorism," 453. Some but not all moralistic terrorism is political
terrorism, or vice versa. "Narcoterrorism" is a special subform of predatory terrorism, not a separate, additional form of terrorism. For this
fundamental distinction at the heart of terrorism as a kind of use of
force or violence for certain ends, I am indebted to Edel's essay.

24. Weinberg and Davis, Introduction, 6. Italics in original. Igor Primoratz
is one other author who recognizes the distinction. In "On the Ethics
of Terrorism," in *Shaping Revolution*, Elspeth Attwooll, ed. (Aberdeen,
1991), 201, he distinguishes the "primary" and "secondary" targets of
terrorism. He adds that sometimes "the same person or group is both
the primary and secondary target." Whether that is possible, especially in any actual cases, is an interesting question.

25. Vetter et al., *Perspectives*, 5. See also Paul Wilkinson, *Political Terrorism* (London, 1974), 12f., for a discussion of what he calls the "criminal variety" of terrorists. He notes that criminal terrorists "resort to

terrorising their victims with the sole object of selfish material gain or of eliminating a possible rival or informer." In other words, their terrorism is either predatory or retaliatory in our sense.

26.   Vetter et al., *Perspectives*, 5.

27.   Ibid., 6.

28.   *House Resolution 2781*, 99th Congress, 1st Session, 1-3. The resolution unforunately equates "terrorism" with "terror"; see later.

29.   *Convention for the Suppression of Unlawful Seizures of Aircraft* (The Hague, 16 December 1970). See also the CIA definition in Allan S. Nanes, *International Terrorism*, Congressional Research Service (Washington, DC, 1985), the *Convention for the Suppression of Unlawful Acts Against the Safety of Civil Aviation* (Montreal, 23 December 1971), and *Convention on the Prevention and Punishment of Crimes Against International Protected Persons, Including Diplomatic Agents*, adopted by the UN General Assembly, 14 December, 1973. See further, Harriet Culley, *International Terrorism*, Bureau of Public Affairs, U.S. Department of State (Washington, DC, August 1985).

30.   *Terrorism, An Introduction* (Belmont, CA, 1991), p. 5. Italics added.

31.   In his *Terrorism and the Liberal State*, 2nd. ed. (London, 1986), 59, Wilkinson briefly defines political terrorism as "the systematic use of murder and destruction, and the threat of murder and destruction in order to terrorize individuals, groups, communities or governments into conceding to the terrorists' political demands." Unfortunately this is not a neutral definition, since "murder," if not also "destruction," has very strong condemnatory connotations.

32.   Wilkinson, *Political Terrorism*, 11. And see 11ff. for a comparative discussion of terror and terrorism.

33.   Quoted from ibid., 13.

34.   Ibid., 17.

35.   Ibid., 17-18.

36.   Likewise moralistic and some retaliatory terrorism by terrorist states and state-sponsored terrorism. Iran-sponsored terrorism is a clear example of the latter.

37.   An example of a work that appears to equate "terror" and terrorism is *Terror and Urban Guerrillas: A Study of Tactics and Documents*, Jay Mallin, ed. (Coral Gables, FL., 1971). Mallin (3f., passim) considers terrorism as a form of guerrilla warfare.

38.   Edel, "Notes on Terrorism," 458.

39.   Examples of essentialist concepts are the various geometrical concepts, such as that of triangle, square, circle in plane geometry. Ludwig

Wittgenstein first drew attention to "family resemblance" concepts in, for example, his famous analysis of what he called "language games" and what we call "games." See his *Philosophical Investigations* (Oxford, 1963), 31e-32e.

40.   Weinberg and Davis, Introduction, 7-8. Italics added.

41.   Ibid., 11.

Chapter 2

The Morality of Terrorism

I

Although the literature on terrorism is constantly growing, very little has been written about the morality of terrorism; perhaps because the writers take it for granted that terrorism is a scourge, always morally reprehensible and wrong: note for instance the common equation of terrorism with murder. Only a mere handful of articles by Anglo-American philosophers (some of which will be referred to in this chapter) and only one book to date by a philosopher, Burleigh Taylor Wilkins' *Terrorism and Collective Responsibility*[1] deals with it at all. The same is true of books on terrorism by nonphilosophers. Only two books I know of are devoted to the subject: *The Morality of Terrorism: Religious and Secular Justifications*, edited by David C. Rapaport and Yonah Alexander,[2] and *Political Murder by Franklin Lord*[3] (note the title). Paul Wilkinson includes a short section entitled "Terrorism and Criminality" *in his Terrorism and the Liberal State.*[4] He begins by noting[5] that

> Because terrorists, by definition, follow a systematic policy of terror . . . their acts are analogous to crimes . . . . In most legal systems the typical acts of terrorist groups (such as bombings, murders, kidnaping, wounding and blackmail) constitute serious offences under the prevailing codes. Without exception murder is punishable under the legal code of all states. As terrorism involves systematic cold-blooded murder it is particularly repugnant to the Judaeo-Christian tradition and to all societies which are deeply infused with human values.

This is not a very auspicious beginning for a moral evaluation of terrorism. From the fact that terrorist acts, including the killing of immediate victims, are prohibited in many if not all municipal legal systems, it does not follow that some or all such acts are *morally* wrong. Calling terrorist killings "murder" begs the complex ethical issues involved, even if one subscribes to the traditional Natural Law theory of law or to a contemporary form of that theory: that is, if one supposes that a putative law is law proper only if it is just or moral. Even then the putative immorality of terrorist acts must first be established for the Natural Law legal philosopher or jurist to accept the municipal laws that outlaw terrorist acts as *bona fide* laws rather than (in Aquinas' graphic description) "violence."[6]

Wilkinson distinguishes four "special cases of exception" to the still widely held "divine injunction" against murder. These special cases or exceptions, according to him, are: "(i) murder committed in the course of a just war on behalf of one's country . . . , (ii) judicial execution in punishment for the crimes of murder or treason . . . , (iii) murder committed in the course of a just rebellion against tyrannical rule or foreign conquest; and (iv) in self-defense against violent attack."[7] He adds: "Clearly there is a world of difference between justification for specific acts of murder and justification for a systematic policy of indiscriminate murder as a means to a political end."[8] (We can add "predatory," "retaliatory" and "moralistic/religious" to "political end.")

Whether at a minimum some terrorist acts committed in the course of a just war or rebellion are morally justified is an important question and will be discussed in this chapter in relation to just war theory, as well as in Chapter 4 in relation to liberationist revolutionary movements. But no terrorist killings or other forms of violence against the immediate victims can fall under—and so can be justified as—"self-defense"; and clearly, terrorist killing cannot be normally regarded as "judicial execution in punishment for the crimes of murder or treason." Wilkinson is therefore right that terrorist killings cannot be morally justified as falling under exceptions (i) and (iii). I am assuming for the sake of argument that in certain circumstances killing in self-defense and in judicial execution are morally justifiable.

I say that no act of terrorist killing can be *normally* considered as judicial execution because a terrorist *state* that practices terrorism from above against its own citizens may conceivably execute its victims "judicially." That is, if such "execution" is in accord with the country's municipal law. Even then such executions would be murder unless one adopts a radical legal positivist theory of law.[9] On a Natural Law theory of jurisprudence the execution *would* be murder, hence unlawful, if terrorism from above is immoral. Thus we come back to the fundamental question of the morality of terrorism, in this case terrorism from above.

Executions by kangaroo courts, whose victims are framed or otherwise denied the rights and protections of a just penal system, are clearly reprehensible and must be automatically eliminated from the the present inquiry into the morality of terrorism. Two examples of such horrible miscarriages of justice in living memory are Joseph Stalin's infamous purges in the 1930s, and the "disappearances" of thousands of people in South American countries during the 1970s. But the "judicial" executions practiced even by a terrorist state cannot be dismissed *en masse*, as cold blooded murder, without examination.[10] Assuming that capital punishment is morally justifiable, it is just conceivable—though unlikely in the extreme—that the courts in a terrorist state may on occasion justly execute properly convicted murderers.

In the book referred to above, Wilkinson condemns the "deliberate choice of systematic and indisciminate murder as their [the terrorists'] sole or principal means of struggle",[11] even if they claim, "as they commonly do, that they are waging a just war or just rebellion in terms of the classical criteria laid down by theologians and moral philosophers."[12] He adds that it is "a logical absurdity to try to justify terrorism in terms of an ethic founded on the sanctity of individual human life."[13]

Wilkinson next considers the supposed "higher 'revolutionary morality' which transvalues everything in terms of the revolutionary struggle," according to which terrorists claim to act.[14] His point is that terrorism is "a moral crime, a crime against humanity, an attack not only on our security, our rule of law, and the safety of the state, but on civilized society itself."[15] Once again he rests his conclusion on "Western Judaeo-Christian, liberal and humanist values, and the ethical and legal systems that have been shaped by this tradition."[16]

Finally, Wilkinson notes the existence of what he calls "revolutionary crimes against humanity. Revolutionary terrorists are those who choose to devote themselves to the macabre specialisms of revolutionary criminality."[17]

Since the central thesis of this chapter and of Chapter 4, and a main thesis of this book is that all types and forms of terrorism are always wrong, I wholeheartedly agree with Wilkinson and all others who condemn terrorism. But Wilkinson's highly suggestive arguments are too sketchy as they stand. What is required are more systematic arguments, particularly as the view that terrorism is always wrong is not universally accepted. True, some who practice or who defend what their critics call terrorism refuse to consider it so at all. They call it "freedom fighting,"[18] implying that terrorism is either universally wrong or wrong in certain instances. On the other hand some philosophers, including some moral philosophers, either defend certain forms of terrorism, or terrorism in certain special circumstances.

Terrorism and Just War Theory

The traditional conditions of a just war are of two sorts: conditions of justified going to war (*jus ad bellum*) and conditions of the just prosecution of a war in progress (*jus in bello*). One of the fundamental conditions of the latter kind is that

> The destruction of life and property, even enemy life and property, is inherently bad. It follows that military forces should cause no more destruction than is strictly necessary to achieve their objectives.(Notice that the principle does not say that whatever is necessary is permissible, but that everything permissible must be necessary). This is the principle of necessity: that *wanton* destruction is forbidden. More precisely, the principle of necessity specifies that a military operation is forbidden if there is some alternative operation that causes less destruction but has the same probability of producing a successful military result.[19]

Another fundamental condition is the principle of discrimination or noncombatant immunity, which prohibits the deliberate harming—above all the killing—of innocent persons. In "Just War Theory" William O'Brien defines that condition as the principle that "prohibits direct intentional attacks on noncombatants and nonmilitary targets",[20] and Douglas Lackey, in *The Ethics of War and Peace*, characterizes it as "the idea that

. . . civilian life and property should not be subjected to military force: military force must be directed only at military objectives."[21] A third fundamental condition is the principle of proportion, as "applied to discrete military ends."[22] That condition is defined by O'Brien as "requiring proportionality of means to political and military ends."[23] Or as Lackey states it, it is the idea that "the amount of destruction permitted in pursuit of a military objective must be proportionate to the importance of the objective. This is the *military* principle of proportionality (which must be distinguished from the *political* principle of proportionality in the *jus ad bellum*)."[24]

My contention, which I shall justify in Chapter 3, is that these three principles, duly modified or adapted, are analogically applicable to all the types of terrorism distinguished in Chapter 1, and that they are flagrantly violated by them. Indeed, all but the moralistic/religious type of terrorism violate a further condition of just war theory. I refer to the first and most important condition of *jus ad bellum* and one of the most important conditions of a just war in general: the condition of just cause. This condition is defined by Lackey as the rule ". . . that the use of military force requires a just cause," that is, a "wrong received."[25] As he notes regarding discussions held since the U.N. Charter was framed, "Members of the United Nations have continued to assume that just cause consists only in self-defense, but 'self-defense' has come to be understood as a response to aggression."[26] The definition of 'aggression' adopted by the General Assembly on December 14, 1974, consists of seven articles. These articles, Lackey points out, count as aggression "only military acts that might substantially affect the physical security of the nation suffering aggression. The only violation of rights that merits the unilateral use of force by nations is the physically threatening use of force by another state." Lackey observes that the definition excludes "attacks on citizens abroad, assaults on nonmilitary ships and aircraft on the high seas, and the seizure of property of aliens."[27]

Of the four main types of terrorism, predatory, retaliatory and nonmoralistic/religious terrorism clearly run afoul of the just cause condition, understood—in a nutshell—as the self-defensive use of force. Conceivably only some acts of moralistic and moralistic-political/religious terrorism can satisfy that condition. It is clear that the former three types of terrorism violate that condition.

Let us begin with predatory terrorism, terrorism motivated by greed. Like "ordinary" acts of armed robbery, of which it is the terrorist counterpart, predatory terrorism is a crime and is morally wrong. Both cause terror and indiscriminately hurt whoever happens to be where they strike. Indeed, hostage-taking by armed robbers in hopes of escaping unscathed by forcing the authorities to give them a getaway car or plane is an additional similarity to terrorism. It can even be regarded as predatory terrorism itself, particularly if it is systematic and not a onetime affair, since both political and moralistic terrorism tend to be systematic, as Wilkinson notes in relation to political terrorism. Even then, armed robbery involving hostage-taking, must be distinguished from the kind of armed robbery that political or moralistic terrorists may indulge in to raise money for their particular political/moralistic/religious ends.

Nonetheless, bona fide predatory (and even retaliatory) terrorism is often unsystematic; like ordinary armed robbery, it may also be a one-time thing. Some well-known terrorist airplane hijackings in the United States for monetary gain have been one-time incidents, although in all but one instance I know of, that was simply because the hijackers were apprehended!

Like predatory terrorism, retaliatory terrorism may or may not be systematic. International terrorism usually includes a systematic policy of retaliation against a hated, enemy state or its citizens. A notorious example a few years ago was the retaliatory terrorism against the United States and its interests, sponsored by Libya, Syria, and/or Iran.

More important for the present discussion, retaliatory terrorism violates, among other moral rules, the just cause condition and the principles of justice, and is consequently wrong. For what is retaliation but another (more euphemistic?) word for revenge, which is incompatible with self-defense as well as due process. That is no less true in war, if retaliatory terrorism is practiced by a country in its efforts to defend itself against aggression. For example, if an attempt is made on the life of the aggressor country's head of state by agents of the victim state in retalation for attacks on its territory, the assassination attempt would be (a) an act of *terrorism* if it is *intended* to pressure the aggressor's military to end the aggression. But despite its *goal* and the victim's perception of it as part of its national self-defense, it remains (b) an act of retaliation, not an act of self-defense.

What I have said about predatory and retaliatory terrorism in relation to just cause applies to nonmoralistic political terrorism, to terrorism whose political goals are *not* moral. An example is when a revolutionary group commits acts of terrorism against a legitimate, democratically elected government it wants to overthrow out of lust for power.

By definition, moralistic terrorism satisfies just cause if "just cause" is interpreted broadly to mean a morally justifiable cause, for example, political terrorism strictly as part of a national liberation movement against a foreign occupier or indigenous oppressive regime. It *may* also satsfy the condition of right intention. Consequently, I shall turn to the other two conditions of just war I mentioned earlier, to ascertain whether even such terrorism can be morally justifiable.

Principle of Necessity and Terrorism

The principle of necessity states that "*wanton* destruction [in war] is forbidden. More precisely, the principle . . . specifies that a military operation is forbidden if there is some alternative operation that causes less destruction but has the same probability of producing a successful military result."[28] *Pace* Lackey, who regards it as a more precise form of the condition, it is distinct from, although closely related to, the principle that wanton destruction is forbidden in war. If a war *is* a last resort, it would follow that the destruction of life and property is necessary, not wanton. And if it is necessary, it *is* a last resort.

It is clear that predatory terrorism is always a wanton destruction of life or property, and the same is true of retaliatory terrorism; however, the concept of "last resort" is inapplicable to them. If Iran had chosen to sue the United States for compensation or reparation at the International Court of Justice at the Hague, for the shooting down an Iranian airbus during the Iraq-Iran war, that would have constituted a peaceful, nonviolent *alternative* to any terrorist retaliation against the United States Iran may have sponsored in its aftermath, such as the destruction of Pan Am Flight 103 over Lockerbie, Scotland, which some believe was instigated and financed by Iran and implemented by a notorious Palestinian terrorist. (The United States has steadfastly held Libya, and possibly Syria, responsible for that atrocity.) Logically, retaliation on the one hand and reparation, compensation, or restitution, or other peaceful ways of undoing or rectifying a wrong, are horses of very different colors.

Principle of Discrimination and Terrorism

In many acts of terrorism some or all of the immediate victims and/or victimized are innocent persons, in no way morally connected with or in any degree responsible for the wrong moralistic terrorism is intended to help rectify, hence for the physical or mental harm that the terrorists inflict on them. In predatory terrorism the immediate victims and the victimized are, almost without exception, innocent persons. That is also often true of retaliatory terrorism, at least as far as the immediate victims are concerned. Two very tragic examples in recent memory are the hijacking of the *Achille Lauro*, and the destruction of the Pan Am plane over Lockerbie. In political and political-moralistic terrorism, whether in wartime or in time of peace, some of the immediate victims or some of the victimized are likely to be innocent persons; but some may be noninnocents, such as members (especially high-ranking members) of the military, who are morally responsible for the real or imagined wrong that triggers the terrorism.

The problem of distinguishing innocent and noninnocent persons in relation to different types and forms of terrorism, except terrorism in war, is on the whole less difficult than the much-vexed corresponding problem in relation to war. My position, *mutatis mutandis* in relation to war, simply stated, is this: (1) "Innocence" and "oninnocence" refer to *moral* innocence and noninnocence, relative to the particular acts, types, or forms of terrorism *T*. (2) Innocence and noninnocence are a matter of degree. (3) A perfectly innocent person is one who

has no moral responsibility, *a fortiori*, no causal responsibility
at all, for any wrong that gave rise to *T*. A paradigmatically
noninnocent person is someone who has an appreciable degree of moral, hence direct or indirect causal responsibility
for the wrong, triggering *T*.[29] Between that extreme and paradigmatic noninnocents there would be, theoretically, cases of
decreasing moral responsibility corresponding to decreasing
degrees of causal responsibility. Here the targets would be
noninnocent in some but lesser degree than in paradigmatic
cases of noninnocence. (4) Moral responsibility may be direct
or indirect, by virtue of a person's direct or indirect role in *T*'s
causation—where *T* is triggered or has its root cause(s) in some
real injustice or wrong. The degree of a person's innocence
may therefore also vary in that way. Everyone whose actions
are a proximate cause of the wrong is noninnocent in a higher
degree than those whose responsibility for it is indirect. In
particular cases it is always possible in principle to ascertain
whether an individual is, causally, directly involved. Generally
it is also actually possible, although often quite difficult, to do
so in practice. Ascertaining who is indirectly responsible and
who is not at all responsible is another matter. Since we are
mainly concerned with the theoretical problem of the morality of terrorism, that is not too disquieting. But it is of the
essence from the point of view of would-be terrorists and that
of the law—unless the terrorists happen to be deranged and
target innocent individuals or groups they imagine to be morally responsible for the grievances they are out to avenge or
redress. Further, the very life of some individuals may depend
on the potential terrorists' ability to distinguish innocent from
noninnocent persons or groups. Political, retaliatory, or moralistic terrorists, driven by passion or paranoia, often baselessly
enlarge, sometimes to a tragically absurd extent, the circle of
alleged noninnocent persons. They sometimes target individuals, groups or whole nations having only a tenuous relation,
often of a completely innocent kind, to those who have wronged
their compatriots or ancestors, stolen their land, and so on.
The example given earlier of terrorists striking at the high-
ranking officials of governments whose predecessors committed crimes against their people, illustrates this. Another example is terrorism targeting innocent persons presumed to be

guilty by association, simply because they happen to be of the same race, nationality, or religion, or enjoy the same ethnic heritage as those deemed responsible for the hurt.

An extreme, horrifying kind of justification of the targeting of completely innocent persons was brought to my attention by Anthony O'Heare.[30] It involves the justification one sometimes hears of the killing of holidaymakers, tavelers, and others, in Israel and other terrorist targets, "on the ground that . . . the very fact that they were contributing to the economy and morale of the targeted country [unwittingly] implicated them." As O'Heare comments, that defense is "a disgusting piece of casuistry." Its implications, I might add, are so far-reaching as to be positively frightening. If the travelers or holidaymakers were guilty of a crime against, say, the Palestinian people, as is claimed, then by parity of reasoning all individuals, institutions, groups or peoples, all countries or nations that have any kind of economic dealings with Israel and so contribute to its economy would likewise be guilty of a crime against the Palestinian people and so may be justifiably targeted! But then why exempt those *Arabs* who live in Israel and even those *Palestinians* residing in the West Bank or in the Gaza Strip who are employed in Israel—indeed, all those who spend any amount of money there—from guilt?

Finally, to be able to protect individuals against terrorism, law enforcement agencies as well as governments in general need to be able to protect individuals against terrorism, need to make reliable predictions about who is a likely target of known terrorist organizations. Yet in few other kinds of coercison or other uses of force is the element of unpredictability and surprise greater or the strikes more impelled by emotion and passion than in terrorism. This problem will be later taken up again in a discussion of responses to terrrorism.

Principles of Proportion and Terrorism

In addition to its violation of the moral principles considerd above, terrorism may appear to violate two other principles of just war theory: (1) the *political* principle of proportion of *jus ad bellum* and (2) the *military* principle of proportion of *jus in bello*. The former is stated by William O'Brien as requiring that "the good to be achieved by the realisation of the war aims be proportionate to the evil resulting from the war."[31] And "the calculus of proportionality in just cause [that is, the political purpose, *raison d'etat*, "the high interests of the state"] is to the total good to be expected if the war is successful balanced against the evil the war is likely to cause."[32] Lackey describes the political principle of proportionality as stipulating that "a war cannot be just unless the evil that can reasonably be expected to ensue from the war is less than the evil that can reasonably be expected to ensue if the war is not fought."[33]

The military counterpart of the political principle is described by Lackey as the idea that "the amount of destruction permitted in pursuit of a military objective must be proportionate to the importance of the objective. It follows from the military principle of proportionality that certain objectives should be ruled out of consideration on the ground that too much destruction would be caused in obtaining them."[34]

As in the case of war, the main problem facing any attempt to apply the *political* principle of proportion to terrorism is the difficulty of reaching even the roughest estimate of the total expected good *vis-a-vis* the total evil likely to be caused by a series of connected acts of political or *moralistic/religious* terrorism. The crudest estimates of the expected good of some political-moralistic/religious cause against the suffering or death of even one victim or victimized person are exceedingly difficult to come by. And if we turn from isolated acts of political-moralistic/religious terrorism to a whole series of such acts extending over a period of years or decades, as with Arab or IRA terrorism, the task becomes utterly hopeless. For how can we possibly measure the expected good resulting from the creation of, for example, an independent Catholic Northern Ireland or a Catholic Northern Ireland united with the Irish Republic, and compare it with the overall evil likely to be the lot of the Ulster Protestants in such an eventuality or on different scenarios of their eventual fate—then add the latter evil to the evils consisting in and consequent upon all the acts of terrorism that are supposed to help realise the desired good end? I see no possible way in which these factors can be quantified, hence added or subtracted.[35]

It seems then that we cannot ascertain whether political or moralistic/religious terrorism sometimes or always violates the political principle of proportion. However, it is a patent fact that no political or moralistic/religious terrorist movement in this century—whether Palestinian, Lebanese, Libyan, Syrian, Iranian, Irish, or Algerian—has succeeded in realizing its ultimate or overall political or moralistic objectives. Moreover, these movements have no more chance of success in the future than they have had so far. Palestinian terrorism is typical. Since, in Israel and the West, terrrorism is almost synonymous with murder, it is not surprising that instead of helping the eminently just Palestinian cause, Palestinian acts of terrrorism (as distinguished from Palestinian resistance, e.g. the intifada) from the very start have hurt that cause almost beyond repair. Not only has terrorism failed to win the Palestinians their human and other rights or brought them any closer to selfdetermination: it has created strong public sympathy in the West for Israel and turned public attitudes strongly against the Palestinians, or at least their leadership, and has further increased Israeli security concerns.[36] This does enable us, I think, to conclude after all that the preceding types of terrorism are indeed in serious violation of the political principle of proportion. For the result of tallying the evils of terrorist acts in human pain and suffering, death and destruction, against the nonexistent overall benefits leaves a huge surplus of unmitigated evil on the negative side. I refer not only to the evil inflicted by the terrorists upon their victims and the victimized but also the evil they draw upon themselves and their families by risking loss of life, limb, or liberty in ultimately futile pursuit of their dangerous and violent objectives.

We now turn to the military principle of proportionality—in O'Brien's words, the principle that "a discrete military means . . . when viewed independently on the basis of its intermediate military end (*raison de guerre*), must . . . be proportionate . . . to that military end for which it was used, irrespective of the ultimate end of the war at the level of *raison d'etat*."[37] This principle, applied to discrete military means, O'Brien observes, is in line with the law of Nuremberg, which judged the "legitimacy of discrete acts of the German forces, . . . inter alia, in terms of their proportionality to intermediate military goals, *raison de guerre. . . .* It was a reasonable way to evaluate the substance of the allegations that war crimes had occurred."[38]

The present form of the principle *can* be applied, *mutatis mutandis,* to discrete acts of terrorism provided that their probable intermediate results can be roughly assessed. For example, in evaluating the morality of the *Achille Lauro* seajacking, the short-term and intermediate "political" gains the terrorists expected to receive must be weighed, if possible, against the killing of an innocent passenger and the terrorism visited on the other passengers on board. It can be safely said that apart from the damage the seajacking did to the PLO and to the Middle East peace process as a whole, whatever benefit the seajackers expected to reap from their acts,[39] such as publicity and the dramatization of the plight of the Palestinians under Israeli military rule in the occupied territories, was vastly outweighed by the evils the seajacking resulted in.[40] More important still, the actual and not (as in O'Brien's formulation of the principle) merely the expected outcome of acts of terrorism, good and bad, must be weighed, if possible, against each other. That is, actual proportionality must obtain if, in retrospect, the acts are to be objectively evaluated. But to do so is precisely to assess the outcomes of the acts in terms of consequentialist criteria, and so will be left for later consideration.

The same general factors need to be weighted for the evaluation of other discrete acts of terrorism in relation to the military principle of proportionality; for example, the assassination of members of the Israeli Olympic team in Munich in 1972, the hijacking of TWA flight 847 in Athens, Greece, in 1985, the downing of Pan Am flight 103 over Lockerbie, Scotland, in 1989, and so on.

Terrorism and Human Rights

It can be safely said that the belief that all human beings have a (an equal) human right to life, at least in the minimal sense of a negative right to life—a right not to be unjustly or wrongly killed—is held by anyone who believes in the existence of human rights at all. That idea is also found in the United Nations *Universal Declaration of Human Rights.* Thus, Article 3 states, among other things, that "Everyone has the right to life." The importance of our acknowledging such a universal human right is evident: the protection of human life is the sine qua non of the individual's capacity to realize anything and everything—any and all values—a human being is capable of realizing in relation to himself or herself and others. But even if one does not acknowledge a distinct human right, a right to life as such, I believe that one is forced to acknowledge the existence of some protective norms, such as other human rights and/or principles of fairness and justice, that prohibit, except in very special circumstances, the taking of human life. For instance, justice prohibits the execution of an innocent person for a crime he or she has not committed. Or the moral protection of human life can be placed under the protective umbrella of, for example, a human right to be treated as a moral person rather than be used as an "object."

The special exceptional circumsances I have in mind are those in which the right to life is overridden by stronger moral or other axiological claims. They may include the protection of the equal rights of others, including others' right to life itself (such as in the case of soldiers sent by their country to war, to defend the lives and freedoms of their countrymen against an aggressor nation); or situations where a certain act is (1) the lesser or two evils and (2) violates no one's equal human or other moral rights, or the principles of fairness and justice. For instance, in some instances of passive or active euthanasia, or assisted suicide, such as in the case of terminal patients who are suffering unbearable physical pain [condition (1)] and the euthanasia or assisted suicide fulfils the patient's devout wish and desire to die [condition (2)]. Except in such or similar exceptional cases, the deliberate or the knowing killing of innocent persons is morally wrong.

Elsewhere[41] I have argued that we must acknowledge a fundamental human right of all individuals to be treated as moral persons. Further, that that right includes an equal right of all to be free to satisfy their needs and interests, and to actualize their potentials: that is, to seek to realize themselves and their well-being.[42] In addition, I have argued that all human beings have an equal right to equal opportunity and treatment, to help enable them to realize the aforementioned values, either as part of or as implied by the right to be treated as a moral person.

A universal negative human right to life,[43] hence a right to one's physical and mental security and integrity, can be readily derived from the right to equal treatment and opportunity as a premise, if such a right is acknowledged,[44] as a condition of the very possibility of exercising that right at all or any other moral, legal, or other kind of right or rights, including the right to be treated as a moral person as a whole. The rights to equal treatment and opportunity would be empty or meaningless in practice if not in theory if one's security is not protected. Indeed, given Thomas Hobbes' three principal causes of quarrel in human nature—competition, "diffidence" or desire for safety, and the desire for glory in the absence of the protective norm of the equal human right to life and its reinforcement by law, human existence would tend to exemplify Hobbes' State of Nature. There would be "no arts; no letters; no society; and which is worst of all, continual fear, and danger of violent death; and the life of man, solitary, poor, nasty, brutish, and short."[45]

It is clear that if a negative right to life is assumed, terrorists' killings of their immediate victims—unless they satisfy conditions (1) and (2) above—are always morally wrong. In reality, condition (1) may perhaps be sometimes satisfied, but condition (2) cannot ever be satisfied. In fact all types and forms of terrorism I have distinguished seriously violate the human rights of their immediate victims and the victimized as moral persons.

Treating people as moral persons means treating them with consideration in two closely related ways. First, it means respecting their autonomy as individuals with their own desires and interests, plans and projects, commitments and goals. That autonomy is clearly violated if they are humiliated, coerced and terrorized, taken hostage or kidnapped, and above all, killed. Second, consideration involves "a certain cluster of attitudes, hence certain ways of acting toward, reacting to and thinking and feeling about" people.[46] It includes sensitivity to and consideration of their feelings and desires, aspirations, projects, and goals. That in turn is an integral part of treating their life as a whole—including their relationships and memo-

ries—as a thing of value. Finally, it includes respecting their
"culture or ethnic, religious or racial identity or heritage."[47]
These things are the very antithesis of what terrorism does to
its victims and the victimized.

In sum, terrorism in general violates both aspects of its targets' right to be treated as moral persons. In retaliatory and
moralistic/religious terrorism, that is no less true of those victims or those victimized who are morally responsible in some
degree for the wrong that precipitates the terrorist strike than
of those who are completely innocent of it. In predatory terrorism, the terrorist acts violate the human right of everyone
directly or indirectly hurt by them. For the terrorists the life
of the immediate victims and their human rights matter not in
the least. The same goes for the victimized. The terrorists use
both groups, against their will, simply as means to their own
ends.[48] The matter can also be looked upon in terms of the
ordinary concepts of *justice* and *injustice*. Terror directed
against innocent persons is a grave injustice against them. In
no case is this truer than when terrorists impute to their immediate victims or to the victimized guilt by association. It is
equally true when the victims are representatives of a government one or more of whose precedessors committed large-scale
atrocities, such as attempted genocide, against the terrrorists'
compatriots or ancestors. True, the present government would
be tainted by the original crimes if, to cite an actual case, it
categorically refuses to acknowledge its predecessors' guilt and
take any steps to redress the grievous wrongs. Similarly, if it
verbally acknowledges its predecessors' guilt but washes its
hands of all moral or legal responsibility to make amends to
the survivors of the atrocities or their families, on the ground
that it is a new government, existing decades later than the
perpetrators. Yet only if the targeted representatives of the
present government themselves are in some way responsible
for their government's stand would they be noninnocent in
some degree. Otherwise targeting them from a desire for revenge would be sheer murder or attempted murder.

Whenever the victims or victimized are innocent persons,
terrorism directed against them constitutes a very grave injustice, like "punishing" an innocent person for a crime he or she
has not committed. For in the present sense, justice consists in

one's receiving what one merits or deserves, determined by what one has done or refrained from doing.

It may be argued that some terrorist acts *may* be just punishment for wrongs committed by the immediate victims or the victimized themselves, against the terrorists or persons close to them. But first, punishment cannot be just if founded on a denial of the wongdoer's human as well as other rights. Second, a vast difference exists between terrorist "punishment" and just legal punishment, which presupposes the establishment of guilt by a preponderance of the evidence. By definition, terrorists do not and cannot respect the legal protections and rights of the victims and the victimized, but erect themselves as judges and jury—and executioners—giving the "accused" no opportunity to defend themselves or be defended by counsel against the terrorists' allegations, let alone the possibility of defending themselves physically against their assailants.[49] This is a further corollary of the terrorists' denial of the moral and legal rights of the victims and victimized.

These strictures apply equally to terrorism from above and from below. The fact that in the former case the terrorist "organization" is the government itself or some arm of government (e.g., its secret police), and that the terrorism is practiced against those of its own citizens it considers dangerous or subversive, does not morally change the situation. It is terrorism by any other name. Such for instance was the situation in Brazil (in the 1960s), Argentina (in the 1970s), Colombia (in the 1980s), and in other Latin American countries when right-wing, anticommunist death squads killed or executed thousands of people suspected of leftist sympathies. In some countries "church and human rights organizations have been particularly hard-hit."[50]

To sum up. The discussion of the nature of terrorism in Chapter One prepared the way for the central question of this chapter: whether terrorism is ever morally right, morally justifiable. To answer that question two kinds of ethical principles/rules were deployed, (A) applicable human rights, and (B) applicable just war principles/rules. A third principle, (C) the application of consequentialist, specifically act- and rule-utilitarian principles/rules to terrorism has been left to Chapter 4. On both (A) and (B), terrorism in general, in all its various types and forms, was found to be always wrong.

Since predatory and retaliatory terrorism, like predation and retaliation in general, are patently wrong, the inquiry was focused on political and moralistic/religious terrorism, which are held by some—with apparent plausibility—to be, in certain circumstances, morally justifiable. However, it was argued that terrorism of both types is wrong, since both violate certain basic human rights and applicable just war principles or rules.

Notes

1. Burleigh Taylor Wlkins, *Terrorism and Collective Responsiblity* (New York, 1992). Wilkins' arguments are examined below, in appendix to Chapter 4.

2. David C. Rappaport and Yonah Alexander, eds., *The Morality of Terrorism: Religious and Secular Justifications* (New York, 1983).

3. Franklin Lord, *Political Murder* (Cambridge, MA, 1985).

4. Paul Wilkinson, *Terrorism and the Liberal State*. 2nd ed. (London, 1986).

5. Ibid., 65-66.

6. The same is even more obvious in relation to legal positivism, including the somewhat attenuated form of it advocated by H.L.A. Hart, since for legal positivism the validity of a law is logically or conceptually independent of its morality, its moral goodness or badness.

7. Wilkinson, *Terrorism and the Liberal State*, 66. The word "killing" should be substituted for "murder" in (i)—(iv), since—as the word is normally used—murder includes the concept of unlawfulness and moral wrongness.

8. Ibid.

9. I say "radical legal positivist theory" since H.L.A. Hart, for example, the leading positivist in the Anglo-American world today, accepts what he calls "the core of good sense in the doctrine of Natural Law"—what he calls "the minimum [moral] content of natural law." Hart, *The Concept of Law* (New York, 1961), ch. 9.

10. The way in which particular terrorist states used or may use their municipal legal systems as instruments of terrorism against their own peoples or against segments of them, deserves serious attention. But it is beyond the scope of the present work.

11. Wilkinson, *Terrorism and the Liberal State*, 66.

12. Ibid.

13. Ibid. Despite its alleged absurdity, such an attempt will be considered in Chapter 4, in order to ascertain whether a rule-utilitarian justification of *any* form of political-moralistic/religious terrorism is possible.

14. A striking similarity may be noted between this claim—to the extent that terrorists in fact do make the claim—and Raskolnikov's theory of crime in Dostoevsky's *Crime and Punishment*. On that theory the "extraordinary," Napoleonic or "bronze" man is that rare individual who

is above and beyond conventional morality and law, for whom "every-thing"—all that is conventionally considered to be crime—is permit-ted. For these "crimes"—if they can be considered crimes—are com-mitted solely for the benefit of humankind.

15.   Wilkinson, *Terrorism and the Liberal State*, 66.

16.   Ibid.

17.   Ibid., 67.

18.   See Chapter 5.

19.   Douglas P. Lackey, *The Ethics of War and Peace* (Englewood Cliffs, NJ, 1989), 59. Italics in original.

20.   William O'Brien, "Just-War Theory," in Burton M. Leiser *Liberty, Jus-tice, and Morals*, 2nd ed. (New York, 1979), 39. This section is in large measure reproduced from sections III–V of Haig Khatchadourian, "Terrorism and Morality," *Journal of Applied Philosophy*, 5, no. 2 (1958): 134-143.

21.   Lackey, *Ethics*, 59.

22.   Ibid., 37.

23.   Ibid., 30.

24.   Ibid., 59. Italics in original.

25.   Ibid., 33.

26.   Ibid., 34.

27.   Ibid., 35.

28.   Lackey, *Ethics*, 59. Italics in original.

29.   What constitutes an "appreciable degree" of moral responsibility would of course be a matter of controversy.

30.   Private communication to the author.

31.   O'Brien, "Just War Theory," 37.

32.   Ibid.

33.   Lackey, *Ethics*, 40.

34.   Ibid., 59.

35.   For the special significance of this in relation to revolutionary terror-ism, see Chapter 4.

36.   A personal note: My own moral condemnation of terrorism and my conviction that it was bound to hurt rather than help the Palestinian

cause led me, soon after the first Palestinian skyjacking, to send an open letter to the PLO leadership. In the letter I pointed these things out and pleaded that the PLO put an end to such acts. For rather obvious reasons the Beirut publication to which I sent the letter could not publish it.

37. O'Brien, "Just-War Theory," 37.

38. Ibid., 38.

39. One of the seajackers stated after being captured that the original objective was a suicide mission in Israel. That objective, of course, was not realized.

40. Note that the question whether the capture, trial, and almost certain punishment of the seajackers and others implicated in the act is to be judged a good or an evil to be added to one or the other side of the balance sheet, partly depends for its answer on the evaluation of the act itself as morally justified or unjustified. I say "partly depends" because the legal implications of the act are also relevant.

41. Haig Khatchadourian, "Toward a Foundation for Human Rights," *Man and World*, 18 (1985): 219-240, and "The Human Right to be Treated as a Person," *Journal of Value Inquiry*, 19 (1985): 183-195.

42. Khatchadourian, "The Human Right," passim.

43. As distinguished from a positive human right to life, which includes— over and above the right not to be physically hurt or killed—a right to a minimum standard of welfare.

44. Such a right can also be derived from John Rawls' first and second principles of justice in *A Theory of Justice* (Cambridge, MA, 1971). *Indeed, the right to equal opportunity is part of his first principle.*

45. Thomas Hobbes, "Self-Interest," in *Great Traditions in Ethics*, 5th ed., Ethel M. Albert et al., eds. (Belmont, CA, 1984), 134. Reprinted from *Leviathan*. I should add that Hobbes himself regarded self-preservation as the first law of (human) nature, and that his social contract, the creation of the "Leviathan" of civil and political society, is intended to provide, inter alia, safety and security.

46. Khatchadourian, "The Human Right," 192.

47. Ibid.

48. Cf. Abraham Edel's condemnation of terrorism on Kant's principle that "people ought to be treated as ends in themselves and never as means only. Terrorists necessarily treat human beings as means to the achievement of their political, economic, or social goals." Quoted by Burton M. Leiser in his introduction to the section on terrorism in his *Values in Conflict* (New York, 1981), 343.

49.   See Haig Khatchadourian, "Is Political Assassination Ever Morally Justified?" in *Assassination*, Harold Zellner, ed. (Boston, 1975), 41-55, for similar criticism of political assassination.

50.   Leonard B. Weinberg and Paul B. Davis, *Introduction to Political Terrorism* (New York, 1989), 72.

Chapter 3

Justification of the Just War Principles Used

I

In evaluating terrorism in Chapters 2 and 4, and "freedom fighting" in Chapter 5, and anti- and counterterrorism in Chapter 6, I appeal to three kinds of ethical considerations: (1) applicable conditions or principles/rules of just war theory, adapted to terrorism, freedom fighting, and anti- and counterterrrorism; (2) the protective norms of human rights; and (3) act- and rule-utilitarian consequentialist considerations. In this chapter I shall attempt to provide a philosophical justification for (1) in terms of consequentialist and/or rights norms. But before I do so, it is necessary to justify the appeal to these conditions/principles themselves to the various types and forms of terrorism, since they are all distinct—and in some significant ways, different from—war. I shall provide a justification for the application of these conditions/principles to "freedom fighting" in Chapter 5.

On the other hand, no attempt will be made to provide a philosophical rationale for (2) and (3), consequently for the principles utitized in justifying the principles or rules of just war theory themselves. With regard to (2), the protective norms of human rights, the interested reader is referred to the relevant writings mentioned in Chapter 2. As for (3), act- and rule-utilitarian consequentialist considerations, any attempt to provide a philosophical rationale for it or for consequentialism in general, however brief, would take us too far afield. But at a minimum the goodness or badness of their outcomes are widely regarded in twentieth century moral philosophy as a main kind of ethical consideration in determining the rightness or wrongness of actions, together with certain other kinds of ethical considerations: motives or intentions; human rights; duties, and principles or fairness and justice.[1]

The appeal to just war theory in the moral evaluation of terrorism can be justified as follows. As a kind of violence, terrorism shares a number of important characteristics with war. Since terrorist acts are intended to realize certain immediate, intermediate, and longrange or ultimate goals for the terrorists and/or those on whose behalf they commit these acts, the principles of right intention and just cause are clearly applicable to them. Since some or all of those they harm—the immediate victims and the victimized—may be either innocent or noninnocent, and since some are deliberately targeted while others are accidentally or unintentionally harmed, the principle of innocent immunity also applies to them. Further, terrorist acts, like war, raise the question of the proportionality or disproportionality of the harm inflicted to the actual or probable benefits for their initiators and those on whose behalf the violence is done; hence the "military" and/or political principles of proportionality also apply. Similarly, the principles of necessity, last resort, and chance of success are applicable to terrorist acts, just as they apply to war and to other kinds of uses of force or violence.

In sum, although terrorism differs significantly from war in being "bifocal," it has enough important similarities to justify the analogical appeal of the aforementioned principles to it, although only those that I believe all types and forms of terrorism fail to satisfy are considered in Chapter 2 in the moral evaluation of terrorism.

Philosophical Rationale for Just-War Rules

As suggested in Chapter 2, a number of *jus ad bellum* and *jus in bello* conditions can be given a consequentialist justification. This I believe is true of: (a) just cause, (b) right intention, (c) necessity, (d) last resort, (e) innocent immunity, (f) proportionality, and (e) chance of victory; it is also true of the condition of just peace. I shall consider these rules in turn, though not always in the order given here.

(a) Just Cause

Broadly conceived, "just cause" in relation to war implies an undeserved "wrong received" by a victim state or people from a belligerent people or state, a wrong which morally entitles the victim state or people to use military force with a view (but only with a view) to undoing the wrong or to preventing further undeserved wrongs to itself. Insofar as it has just cause, the victim's use of military force has a clearly consequentialist rationale. Following twentieth-century standards, I take the definition of "just cause" to be force used in response to aggression, solely for the purposes of national self-defense, as defined in Articles 1-5 and 7 in the Charter adopted by the United Nations General Assembly on 14 December 1974.[2]

It should be noted that the UN definition of "just cause" recognizes the rights of peoples as well as states.[3] Consequently if the (moral) rights of peoples can be somehow derived from the human rights to life and individual freedom of the individual citizens or subjects (by the addition of other relevant premises), a rights rationale of the "just cause" rule can also be provided.

On consequentialist grounds the appeal to (often military) force for national self-defense is strongest whenever the defender is morally just. The consequentialist argument becomes considerably weaker, or may lead to the opposite conclusion, in the case of nations that wrong their own people by denying them even minimal rights and liberties. There, two different sorts of considerations may enter the picture, one consequentialist, the other rights-based. The former would maintain that self-defense is morally justified since the alternative— the international community's moral (and legal) acceptance of aggression against such states—can only lead to international anarchy, given the all-too familiar predatory tendencies of the nation-states.[4]

The rights-based argument logically supplements the foregoing consequentialist argument insofar as the UN declares, in Article 7 of the definition of aggression, "the right to self-determination, freedom, and independence, as derived from the Charter, of *peoples* forcibly deprived of that right . . . particularly under colonial and racist regimes or other forms of

alien domination; nor the right of these peoples to struggle to
that end and to seek to receive support."[5] This clearly allows in
principle, on rights-grounds, for (at least) the internal overthrow of unjust governments or political systems or regimes
by the subject peoples.[6]

(b) Right intention

The condition of right intention can be readily given a
consequentialist rationale. For example, the utilitarian tradition from John Stuart Mill to Brand Blanshard and J.J. Smart
provides a model for a consequentialist treatment of intention
in general by defining "right intention" in terms of the tendency of a right-intentioned agent to perform or strive to perform actions that tend to result in, or are conducive to, overall
good consequences. In contemporary just war theory, right
intention is limited to the intention to national self-defense. In
practice, that means a victim state's going to war (1) if and
only when it is a victim of aggression, (2) to (and only to) protect itself against dominion or conquest rather than, or additionally, to inflict harm (or inflict mortal harm) on the aggressor. Conquering his territory, raping or massacring his people,
and the like would constitute acting out of an evil intention.
Clearly, satisfying conditions (1) and (2) would tend to minimize the inevitable evils of war as compared with the acting
out of greed, lust for power, vengefulness, etc. Where the military powers are unequal, right intention may dictate (3) the
victim's accomodating the aggressor rather than resisting him,
thus sparing itself the humiliation and other grave ills of an
inevitable military defeat.

(c) Necessity, (f) Proportionality, and (d) Last resort

Douglas Lackey rightly argues that the principles of necessity
and military proportionality, "and all the rules of war derived
from these principles, obtain their moral content from the
utilitarian [more precisely, the general consequentialist] conception that it is wrong to destroy the good things of the world,
even good things belonging to enemeies that are waging unjust wars." His reason is that "since the utilitarian code gener-
ates unconditional obligations, which bind regardless of what
others do, it follows on this interpretation that the rules of

proportionality and necessity bind nations, even in conflicts with states that neither acknowledge nor obey the rules of war.[7] Lackey observes that alternative interpretation of "evil"—one, as the violation of rights and, two, as the destruction of value—can result in different moral evaluations of particular wars. Fortunately for our purposes, the differences between the two interpretations are immaterial for the moral evaluation of terrorism, though it would affect the evaluation of rebellions and revolutions, coups d'etat, or other forms of revolutionary activities or freedom fighting. It would not affect the moral evaluation of terrorist acts since on both interpretations these acts violate the principle of proportionality, in its political and military senses. It is immaterial whether the evils of terrorism are understood as violations of rights or as the destruction of value, where the latter is understood as excluding the former. As I shall argue in Chapter 4, the history of the past three decades shows that terrorist acts, including political-moralistic terrorist acts, have invariably produced much more evil than good, that they have in fact added to the evils they were intended to help eliminate. The overall dismal record of Middle Eastern, European, and Latin American terrorism is testimony to this.

The "necessity," "last resort," and "chance of victory" requirements too can be readily justified on consequentialist grounds, most obviously, "chance of victory." If the evidence available to the party with the just cause and other grounds shows that going to war will be unlikely to end in anything other than defeat, it would be wrong as well as utter madness to do so. Going to war would inevitably produce greater overall evil for both sides than, for example, reaching some kind of accommodation—including surrendering to the enemy as a last resort.

Similar consequentialist considerations can be provided in relation to "necessity" and "last resort." Certainly, less evil if not more good will result if the just cause can be realized by peaceful means than by war.

(e) Innocent immunity

The situation is quite different with the principle of innocent immunity in its *traditional, absolute* form. As Lackey explains, "discrimination [or innocent immunity] requires that noncombatants should *never* be chosen targets, *even if* considerably more good than evil could be produced by choosing civilian targets. . . . For this principle, only non-utilitarian [deontological] justifications will do."[8]

Lackey distinguishes "objective" and "subjective" forms of the principle. In its subjective form it prohibits intentional but not unintended albeit knowing targeting of civilians (in the present context, innocent persons) in war. The principle is also sometimes stated, in terms of a distinction from "direct killing," as "indirect killing." In indirect killing, "death is a side effect caused by an act that has some intended effect. Given the distinction, theorists declare that the direct killing of civilians [or innocent persons] in war is always murder; the indirect killing of civilians in the course of military operations aimed at military objectives is regrettable but not murderous."[9]

The more stringent objective principle prohibits the knowing albeit unintended killing of innocent persons in war.

Two sorts of deontological rationales are possible, prima facie rights theory and rule deonological theory.

First, rights theory. It can be seen that in addition to violating their rights, the harming of innocent persons in time of war violates their moral rights, most obviously the human right to life, here minimally understood as the negative right not to be killed.

Like rights theory rule deontologism prohibits the intentional killing of innocent persons if murder is defined, as it is in Catholic moral philosophy, as the intentional or deliberate killing of innocent persons. For example, Elizabeth Anscombe categorically asserts that "murder is the deliberate killing of the innocent, whether for its own sake or as a means to some further end."[10]

Is this identification of the intentional killing of an innocent person with murder morally acceptable? The act-utilitarian's answer is obviously no. For him, the intentional killing of innocent persons is right whenever the act results in a greater balance of good over evil. For instance, whenever it is conducive to the general welfare. Although such consequences may almost never occur in practice, they are always theoretically possible, and on the strength of that fact the act-utilitarian would reject the Catholic position. The distinction between innocent and noninnocent persons, and with it the distinction between intentional and unintentional killing, which is crucial for Catholic moral philosophy, plays a very different role in a utilitarian scheme. For it is morally relevant only when the intentional killing of innocent persons adversely affects the action's overall outcome.

Richard Wasserstrom's position in "On the Morality of War: A Preliminary Inquiry" is representative of the general utilitarian position. He writes: "The strongest argument against war is that which rests upon the connection between the morality of war and the death of innocent persons." The argument states that "it is no less wrong and no more justifiable to kill innocent persons in war than at any other time."[11]

Wasserstrom counters that if the arguments against the intentional killing of innocent persons are meant "to assert an absolutist view," the view

> is a hard one to accept. This is so because it ultimately depends upon too complete a rejection of the relevance of consequences to the moral character of action. It also requires too rigid a dichotomy between acts and omissions. It seems to misunderstand the character of our moral life to claim that, no matter what the consequences, the intentional killing of an innocent person could never be justifiable—even, for example, if a failure to do so would bring about the death of many more innocent persons.[12]

The Doctrine of Double Effect

From what I have said earlier in this and preceding chapters it can be seen that I share Wasserstrom's view regarding the moral relevance of the consequences of our actions.[13] I also agree with his second argument. (It will be recalled that in Chapter 2 I specifically excluded active euthanasia, suicide, and assisted suicide from the precept that the intentional killing of innocent persons is murder.) But a deeper evaluation of the deontological position in question requires a critical examination of the doctrine/principle of double effect. Although the Catholic position prohibits the intentional killing of innocent persons, it allows for the *knowing* albeit *unintended* killing of innocent persons in certain circumstances.

Let me start by stating my own view, which is that the knowing though unintended harming of innocent persons *may* be just as immoral as their intended (and so, knowing) harming. In other words the distinction between (a) knowing but unintended and (b) intended, hence knowing, harming of innocent persons is morally irrelevant. The distinction is also morally irrelevant for the utilitarian except, for example, when the knowledge that innocent persons have been knowingly albeit unintentionally harmed produces in the killer a profound sense of guilt and regret.[14] The latter may be at least part of the reason why Wasserstrom, after objecting to the Catholic position, adds that it does not follow that

> the argument from the death of the innocent is either irrelevant or unconvincing. It can be understood to be the very convincing claim that the intentional *or knowing* killing of an innocent person is always prima facie (in sense 2) wrong. A serious evil is done every time it occurs. Moreover, the severity of the evil is such that there is a strong presumption against its justifiability. The burden, and it is a heavy one, rests upon anyone who would seek to justify behavior that has as a consequence the death of innocent persons.[15]

Since Wasserstrom does not tell us, we are left to guess how he would justify his important last reservation; I suspect his reason would be that a behavior that has as a consequence the death of innocent persons would violate the latters' right to life and other human rights.[16]

The rule "The deliberate killing of innocent persons is murder" is shot through with ambiguity—or more charitably, is glaringly incomplete as stated. It does not say anything about (1) the presence or absence of consent on the part of the person killed, or (2) whether the intention involved is morally good or bad; whether, for example, it is one of compassion or mercy, as in active euthanasia or assisted suicide, or whether it is one of jealousy, envy, greed, or hate, or the like. But there is a crucial reason why (1) and (2) are not made clear or incorporated into the principle: in this type of case, for the Catholic position, consent and the motive's goodness are (at the very least) far outweighed by the act's nature: the fact that it is an act of killing an innocent person. Even if the act of active euthanasia or of assisted suicide were performed out of compassion or love, and even if the patient wishes to die or to be killed, the act would still be murder pure and simple according to that view.

In opposition to that, I hold on both rights and consequentialist grounds that in such extreme cases as terminal AIDs or cancer voluntary active euthanasia *is* morally justified; consequently it is not murder. In addition to the greater good or lesser bad consequences of such acts in extreme cases,[17] the patient's right to life and other human rights are not violated. On the contrary, the patient's wishes are respected. Similar considerations apply to suicide and assisted suicide.

In sum, the unqualified, absolute prohibition against killing innocent persons is, in my view, untenable.

Despite the fact that Catholic moral philosophy and theology assign a secondary role to right intention in the moral evaluation of acts of killing, the concepts of right and wrong intention do play a crucial role. For example they play a crucial role in the principle of double effect, which, if sound, provides in one stroke a philosophical rationale for many or all of the traditional principles of *jus ad bellum* and *jus in bello* themselves.

The standard or canonical form of the principle[18] is described as follows by Father James F. Keenan. He writes:"Faced with morally unacceptable courses of action [i.e., intentional killing of an innocent person], the principle of double effect remedied particular quandaries."[19] Thus

> apart from the question of desirable effects, certain actions falling under these concerns are *absolutely* prohibited as means or as ends. Since the [Catholic] Church's teachings are predominantly teleological, however, *only* in these few instances of absolute, deontological prohibitions does the principle of double effect arise. Only there its purposefulness is understood. The principle is adopted as a means of responding to certain situations in which one mistakenly could understand the possible, though not necessary, effects of an act as identical to the means used. Resolving this problem accounts for the principle's utility and "moralness."

Some authors add a further condition in relation to the "double effect": that the good effect must be independent of the undesirable effect.[20] That condition is satisfied by Keenan's following example, since the mother's survival depends on the uterus' removal, not on the fetus' death. The undesirable effect depends upon (producing) the good effect, not the opposite.

Keenan illustrates the principle as he understands it with the example of a doctor who has a patient in her fourth month of pregnancy, suffering from an adnexal tumor. Since a direct abortion, which is regarded by the Church as the deliberate killing of an innocent person, is absolutely prohibited, the principle "provides that the bleeding uterus may be removed. . . . It argues that the act of removing the uterus has a two-fold [or double] effect, the saving of the mother, and the death of the fetus."[21] Although removal of the uterus would normally result in the fetus' death, as it would normally be in the case of abortion, the principle allows it. In addition to satisfying the principle's other conditions, the fetus' death is an unintended (albeit knowing) effect of the removal of the uterus. The doctor *intends* to save the mother's life, not to kill the fetus—the (normally inescapable) undesirable effect of the uterus' removal. Applied to just war theory, the principle of double effect entails that:

(1) The deliberate killing of innocent persons in war is absolutely prohibited, constitutes murder (*rationale of the absolute principle of innocent immunity*);

(2) If a nation "N" (a) has just cause and (b) wages a defensive war against an aggressor; and if (c) the outcome of "N's" self-defense is on the whole better than its refraining from self-defense (*proportionality as a political principle*); and if (d) the war results (or is likely to result) in the restoration or enhancement of the rights of the belligerent nation and others affected by the war (*just peace*), it follows that:

(3) "N" would be morally justified to fight such a war, including its unintended (albeit knowing) killing of innocent civilians;

(4) provided that "N's" intent is solely to repel the attack, to realize its just cause, not to kill innocent citizens or subjects of the aggressor nation (*right intention*).

On the other hand, if diplomacy is a viable alternative to fighting the aggressor (if its fighting is not *absolutely necessary*), "N's" engaging in war would have worse consequences than not fighting. In that case the principle of double effect would not apply.

The role of "just cause" may be made clearer by noting its logical relation to "right intention": namely, the latter's presupposing the presence of a just cause. In the principle of double effect the just cause is precisely that desirable part of the "double effect" for whose sake the morally permissible action is undertaken.

The Morality of the Principle of Double Effect

As Keenan and Anscombe[22] stress, the linchpin of the principle of double effect is the claim that certain kinds of actions, including the deliberate killing of innocent persons, are absolutely wrong, being prohibited by the Bible. Consequently if the claim that the deliberate killing of innocent persons is shown *not* to be wrong in the case of certain kinds of actions, as I have argued, the principle loses its *raison d'etre* in relation to these kinds of actions even if it remains viable in relation to others. In addition, the principle itself suffers from serious difficulties of its own, as I argued in the article referenced earlier (note 18).

The following discussion takes up further difficulties in the principle.

Unintended and Intended Consequences

As we have seen, an important presupposition of the principle is that an agent is not morally responsible for the *foreseeable* or even *known* undesirable consequences of his or her action, provided that these consequences are unintended. The agent is responsible only for the intended consequences he or she can know, predict or foresee at the time or in general. Assuming for the moment that a *conceptual* difference exists between an action's intended consequences and its unintended but known, predictable, or foreseen consequences—for example, between "direct" and "indirect" killing, or between "death as a means or end" and "death as a side effect"[23]—the distinction is, nonetheless, *morally* irrelevant. Morally speaking it is a distinction without a difference.

The knowing albeit "unintentional" involuntary killing of innocent persons, just as their involuntary "intentional" killing, is morally wrong.[24] It is wrong to bomb an enemy city in a war, rebellion, or coup d'etat, even if it is only intended to destroy the enemy's military installations, garrisons, and the like, just as it is wrong to bomb the city to kill the civilian inhabitants. For in both types of cases the killing of civilians is obviously foreseeable. Likewise, it is wrong for terrorists to explode bombs at airports, bus stations, in restaurants or other public places, when it is perfectly obvious that innocent people will die or be maimed, even when the terrorists can truthfully claim that they did not intend to harm anyone but military personnel or high-ranking members of the government they were targeting.

The underlying reason for my position is this: the agent's intention *is* morally relevant *only* when, given his or her knowledge of the foreseeable outcome, the intention to avoid harming innocent persons *actually leads* him or her to choose a different course of action—one that is *effectively* designed to avoid harming them. If no such action, one that can effectively satisfy his or her right intention, is possible in the circumstances, *inaction* would be the right course of action, as most likely to have the least harmful outcome possible. Ideally, if it is at all possible in the particular situation, the most desirable thing to do would be for the agent to change the prevailing *circumstances* so as to enable him or her actually to realize her right intention.

Objective and Subjective Intention

The foregoing point follows directly from the relation between intention in the morally appropriate sense and the action chosen as a means to the intended end. To see this we have to begin by distinguishing intention as an "objective" fact or phenomenon and intention as a "subjective," psychological fact or phenomenon. The morally significant sense of the word is the "objective" one, defined by what one actually does and not independent of and existing prior to the action performed. The opposite is true of intention as a "subjective" phenomenon, as a putative mental "act." The distinction becomes clearer if we consider that one may ("subjectively") intend to do something "X" yet refrain from doing it without ceasing to intend to do it. That is, a particular intention may exist without it being followed by the intended act or kind of act; the intention persists in the act's absence.[25] (That intention must be distinguished from another possible intention, the intention *not* to perform "X.")

In the objective sense presupposed by the principle of double effect, as Anscombe rightly observes, intention is, so to speak, "embodied," implicit in or necessarily "expressed" by, hence inseparable from, the action performed. As an action of a certain kind, the chosen action itself defines or determines and so constitutes the acid test of the intention's character, its nature as a means to the intended end. It follows that not every possible means to the intended goal can be morally right as a means. That is precisely what I think Anscombe implies in referring to the Pauline doctrine "that we may not do evil that good may come."[26]

I might add that we often get a clearer insight into the nature of our (objective) intentions in a particular past situation by recalling what we actually did as concretly expressive of these intentions.

What I have called the "objective" sense of intention is derived from Anscombe's conception of intention in "War and Murder." But she appeals to it to defend the principle of double effect, not to criticize it. She writes: "It is nonsense to pretend that you do not intend to do what is the means you take to your chosen end. Otherwise there is absolutely no substance to the Pauline teaching that we may not do evil that good may come." (In other words, a good end does not justify just any means to that end.)

My agreement with Anscombe regarding what I have called objective intention does not extend to what I have called subjective intention, since I believe that an ordinary "subjective" sense of intention does exist, although I agree with her that it is a dangerous misconception or misrepresentation to think of intention "as an interior act of the mind which could be produced at will." She regards that idea as the source of the principle's repeated abuse from the Seventeenth century on: "Now if intention is all important—as it is—in determining the goodness or badness of an action, then, on this theory of what intention is, a marvellous way offered itself of making any action lawful. You only had to 'direct your intention' in a suitable way. In practice, this means making a little speech to yourself: 'What I mean to be doing is . . . .'"

What Anscombe says is very important. But it entails—as I said under (a) above)—that in the majority of the kinds of cases to which the principle *is* supposed to apply (to quote myself on the matter) "The heart of the principle . . .—the agent's *subjective* intention to produce only the good and not the foreseen evil by-product—plays no morally significant role at all!"[27] Thus:

> Consider moral dilemmas in which only two morally relevant and significant courses of action are open to the agent, each of which has a double effect. The two available choices would consist in either doing something "X" or in refraining from doing it. . . . The crucial thing here is that only one action-type, "X," can realize a desirable end "G," and only one action-type, "not-X," can realize another desirable end "H." The dilemma obtains because the production of "G" by "X" would be accompanied by the evil by-product "not-H," while the production of "H" by "not-X" would be accompanied by the evil by-product "not-G."

Keenan's example of the pregnant woman suffering from an adnexal tumor again comes to mind here. The only choices open to the woman are either (1) ending her pregnancy by having her uterus removed, or (2) letting the pregnancy continue. I shall assume that (1) would save the mother's life but would result in the fetus' death, and that (2) may save the fetus' life but result in the mother's death. A utilitarian would defend (1) as morally right if in the particular circumstances, or as a rule, he or she judges the mother's life to be a greater good than the fetus' survival. But the agent who applies the principle of double effect has no other choice but to act in *exactly* the same way as the utilitarian, and for the same reasons, that is, by "subjectively" intending to realize, and so by taking the necessary steps to realize, what he takes to be the greater good or the lesser evil in the circumstances. The only difference would lie in his or her description of the operation as "removing an adnexal tumor by removing the uterus" rather than "aborting the fetus"—as the utilitarian would call it. *The subjective intention to produce only the action's good consequences and not its undesirable by-product plays no role at all* in the decision and in the choice of action performed. The morally significant objective intention to maximize the good or minimize the evil possible in the circumstances is precisely what the utilitarian would consider a "good or right intention,"—and would be actually operative in the circumstances.

If morally speaking our intentions are defined by the means we choose to attain our ends, it follows that in the above example only *one* kind of objective intention is possible in the circumstances, inasmuch as only one possible kind of action can save the pregant woman's life, however differently the defenders of the principle of double effect may describe that kind of action and the supposed mental act of intention "behind" it.

The same difficulty about "right intention" arises whenever a procedure or course of action with a double effect is causally necessary to bring about a particular desirable result.

It might be argued that in *all* of the principle's actual applications, where, speaking abstractly, only one permissible kind of action is open to the agent, that course of action can nonetheless always take a variety of *specific forms*, at least one of which *would* be morally permissible. There the subjective intention to avoid harming an innocent person can lead the would-be agent to choose a specific form "S" of action-type "A" which is calculated to realize the desired goal. The subjective intention thus "becomes" a morally relevant objective intention. (More correctly, the objective intention implicit in the action would be qualitatively identical with the subjective intention and would logically correspond to it.)

That, admittedly, is sometimes possible. It is illustrated by an example Anscombe gives to show the difference between an intentional act—an act that aims at a foreseen effect—and an act whose consequences, though foreseen, are unintended. The example is of a doctor who administers a dangerous drug to a patient hoping that it will cure him but with full awareness that it may instead kill him. The champion of the principle of double effect would rightly observe that the doctor would implement his benevolent intention by administering the lowest dosage of the drug that, in his professional opinion, is likely to improve the patient's condition. His administering the drug in that way exemplifies his right intention and distinguishes it from other specific options open to him, such as administering higher doses of the drug. In this example, subjective intention is morally relevant, since it leads the physician to choose a specific action that objectively exemplifies it. The particular subjective and objective intentions actually (qualitatively) coincide.

This "way out" is not possible in all (indeed many) kinds of cases, for example, in relation to the pregnant woman example. In that case removal of the fetus, whether through "direct abortion" or through the uterus' removal, cannot be finessed to reflect or "embody" objectively the (subjective) intention to save the mother's life, not (or not also) to kill the fetus.

The same problem faces the principle of double effect in relation to another of Keenan's examples, the case of a woman with ectopic pregnancy. Keenan writes: "A doctor may choose between shelling the tube by a direct abortion [prohibited] or may remove the defective tube [allowed]."[28] Despite the apparent difference in intention in the two cases, the principle of double effect faces the problem that the two alternative procedures necessarily have a morally crucial common component: the fetus' removal from its mother's body and its death. The fact that both shelling the tube and removing it have that common component, and the same consequences, renders the alleged difference between the putative "right intention" and the "bad intention" inapplicable and, consequently, irrelevant. The procedures involved do not "express" or "reflect" such a putative difference.

Subjective and Objective Innocent Immunity

Two versions, a subjective and an objective version of the principle of noncombatant immunity in wartime, can be distinguished. The more restrictive objective version maintains that the principle is violated if civilians are killed as a result of military operations. The subjective version maintains that the principle is violated if, as a result of military operations, civilians are intentionally killed. The latter is generally understood as indiscriminate attacks on civilians or as the treatment of civilians "as *targets* of military force."[29] Lackey notes that the recent UN interpretation of the principle of civilian immunity "leans toward the subjective version." It states in part that "the deaths of civilians or damage to their property which are side-effects of military operations must be necessary for the achievement of the objective and proportionate to its importance."[30]

If the acid test of intention is the means chosen to the intended end, it follows that the weaker, subjective version of the principle of civilian immunity is untenable, as it is in the case of the principle of double effect, where, as we saw, right intention is supposed to play a crucial role. The more adequate, objective version revolves round the distinction between (1) the knowing or even foreseeable killing of civilians, and (2) their unforeseeable hence unknowing killing. In that version the knowing or foreseeable, though unforeseen, killing of civilians would be wrong, whether the action is a result of deliberate targeting or indiscriminate attacks against civilian centers. This view coincides with the UN's earlier, objective version as well as with American and English municipal criminal law.[31]

Father John C. Ford, in "The Morality of Obliteration Bombing," strongly condemns obliteration bombing in war, and significantly restricts the applicability of the principle of double effect. He maintains that "it is illegitimate to appeal to the principle of the double effect when the alleged proportionate [i.e., just] cause is speculative, future, and problematical, while the evil effect is definite, widespread, certain, and immediate."[32] With that qualification he comes perhaps as close to the objective version of the principle of innocent immunity as is possible without abandoning the principle of double effect. Although he does not go as far as to admit that the knowing, indeed foreseeable killing of innocent persons is always wrong, his qualification restricts morally permissible actions whenever the foreseen or known evil effects exceed the intended good consequences, in the morally relevant ways described.[33]

Conclusion

It may be wondered whether the rejection of the principle of double effect undermines the principles of just war theory as they are utilized in this book in evaluating terrorism, "freedom fighting" and responses to terrorism. Fortunately, as I shall attempt to show, the answer is No, apart from the fact that, as I tried to do earlier in this chapter, adequate con-sequentialist and/or rights-based rationales can be alternatively provided for them.

1. One of the reasons for my rejection of the principle of double effect is its absolute prohibition against the deliberate killing of innocents, which leads its advocates to deny that abor-tion, suicide, assisted suicide, and active euthanasia can be ever moral. In the case of abortion, it leads them to deny that, for example, the removal of the uterus of a pregnant woman suf-fering from adnexal tumor, to save the woman's life, consti-tutes aborting the fetus.

I maintained earlier in this chapter that abortion, suicide, assisted suicide, and passive and active euthanasia, are in my view morally permissible if and when they are free and volun-tary, performed at the subject's or patient's express wish or desire.[33] These conditions are of necessity absent in the case of the deliberate (and unintended but foreseeable) killing of innocents in war, terorism, and other kinds of violence, and so leave the universal principle of innocent immunity intact in relation to them.

2. Again, my view that, contrary to the principle of double effect, one is responsible not only for the intended but also for the foreseeable unintended consequences of one's actions, is perfectly consistent with the principle of innocent immunity, as applied to terrorism in Chapter 2 (as well as applied to "free-dom fighting" in Chapter 5 and to responses to terrorism in Chapter 6).

3. My view that the intention "behind" an action is objec-tively determined by the nature of the action performed or the choice made, is consistent with the principle of right in-tention as I understand it. Nothing in that principle requires "intention" to be interpreted as some kind of subjective, men-tal "act," temporally prior to what one does or refrains from doing.

4. Finally, the rejection of the principle of double effect does not affect the just war principle; it does not utilize competent authority, just peace, and (generally if not always) last resort.

To sum up. This chapter was concerned to provide a ratio-nal justification for the application of certain just war prin-ciples/rules in Chapter 2 to terrorism, and for their subsequent application, in Chapters 5 and 6, to "freedom fighting" and responses to terrorism. A twofold justification of these principles/rules was provided: First, their applicability to terrorism was defended; second, they were themselves shown to be justifiable, with one exception, in terms of certain consequentialist moral principles. That exception was the absolutist principle of innocent immunity, which could only be justified on deontological grounds. A propos of that principle, the concept of intentional (and of knowing albeit unintended) harming or killing of innocents was subjected to critical examination. That in turn led to a critical examination—and rejection—of the Catholic doctrine or principle of double effect, where the abolute prohibition on intentional killing of innocents is crucial.

The chapter ended with a defense of the claim that the rejection of the principle of double effect does not undermine the principles of just war theory, as they are utilized, in this book, in evaluating terrorism, "freedom fighting," and responses to terrorism.

Notes

1. A defense of a pluralistic ethical theory involving, among other things, appeals to caring and responsibility as well as to rights, principles of fairness and justice, and to outcomes, is being developed in a forthcoming work.

2. Douglas Lackey, *The Ethics of War and Peace* (Englewood Cliffs, NJ, 1989), 34-35.

3. Article 51 of the charter states: "Nothing in the present Charter shall impair the inherent right of individual or collective self-defense if an armed attack occurs against a member of the United Nations, until the Security Council has taken the measures necessary to maintain international peace and security." Quoted from Lackey, *Ethics*, 34.

   Note also Article 7 of the definition of aggression: "Nothing in this definition . . . could in any way prejudice the right to self-determination, freedom, and independence, as derived from the Charter, of peoples forcibly deprived of that right." Quoted from Lackey, *Ethics*, 35.

4. Cf. Hobbes. During the Bosnian civil war, a similar consequentialist argument was being urged criticizing the absence of active Western European and American military involvement in Bosnia-Herzegovina to stop the atrocities and "ethnic cleansing"; namely, that not stopping these horrors and not punishing the perpetrators was likely to tempt other countries to follow suit with respect to their own ethnic minorities.

   Of course the difference here is that this example involves outside military intervention to help the victim country defend itself against its neighbor's aggression, rather than the rationale for the latter's own self-defense. But obviously the concept of national self-defense includes the idea of outside help by allies—and under certain conditions, nonallies as well—to fend off aggression.

5. Lackey, *Ethics*, 35. Italics added.

6. A consequentialist argument supplementing that rights argument is also not difficult to construct.

7. Both quotes: Lackey, *Ethics*, 64.

8. Ibid., 65. Italics in original.

9. Ibid., 66.

10. Elizabeth Anscombe, "War and Murder," in War and Morality, Richard Wasserstrom, ed. (Belmont, CA, 1970), 49. See also in the same

work, Fr. John C. Ford, "The Morality of Obliteration Bombing," 15-41.

11. Both quotes: Richard Wasserstrom, "On the Morality of War: A Preliminary Inquiry," in Wasserstrom, *War and Morality*, 94.

12. Ibid., 99.

13. As we shall see, Anscombe and Catholic moral philosophy do assign a significant moral role to consequences, although certainly not to the same extent or in the same way as unrestricted consequentialism.

14. A utilitarian may nevertheless argue that the sense of guilt and the regret would be a good thing if they make people more careful in avoiding the unintentional or even unknowing harming of innocent persons.

15. Wasserstrom "On the Morality of War," 99-100. Note the significant addition of the words I have italicized, which is *not* part of the Catholic position. In Wasserstrom's sense 2 the immorality of deliberately killing persons in war is prima facie not *absolutely* wrong. But he notes (p. 98) that, on that view, "even when special, overriding circumstances do obtain so that an act of [deliberately killing an innocent person] is justifiable, it still involves some quantum of immorality."

16. See the discussion in Chapter 4.

17. I have already noted, in Chapter 3, Hume's classic defense of suicide on consequentialist (as well as on contractual) grounds.

18. In "Is the Principle of Double Effect Morally Acceptable?" *International Philosophical Quarterly*, 28, no. 1[109] (March 1988): 21-30, I criticized four putative versions of the principle of double effect in contemporary philosophical discussion.

19. Fr. James F. Keenan, "Taking Aim at the Principle of Double Effect: A Reply to Khatchadourian," *International Philosophical Quarterly*, 28, no. 2[110] (June 1988): 201-205. This and the following quotation are from p. 202. Italics in the original.

20. In his article (p. 38) Father John Ford suggests the further qualification that "It is illegitimate to appeal to the principle of the double effect when the alleged proportionate cause is speculative, future, and problematical, while the evil effect is definite, widespread, and immediate."

21. Keenan, op. cit., 203.

22. Anscombe, "War and Murder," 50-51, states that in Christian ethic, "There is a large area where what is just is determined partly by a prudent weighing up of consequences. But the prohibitions are bed-

rock, and without them, the Christian ethic goes to pieces. Hence the necessity of the notion of double effect."

23. Lackey, *Ethics*, 66.

24. Note that the morality of aborting a fully-formed fetus in special circumstances, such as when the pregnancy threatens the mother's life, involves complexities that require special consideration.

25. Subjective intention, misconceived as a "private" mental act conceptually independent of the would-be agent's disposition to perform some particular physical act or kind or act and only contingently connected with action, is a corollary of Descartes' psychophysical dualism. The latter suffers from all the ills of the official "ghost in the machine" model of a human person that Gilbert Ryle, Ludwig Wittgenstein, and P. F. Strawson among others have laid to rest. Subjective intention is perhaps more adequately analyzable in dispositional terms, and so is probably not a kind of mental "act" at all, whatever "mental act" may mean.

26. This and the succeeding Anscombe quotes are from her "War and Murder," 51. See also, Haig Khatchadourian, "Self-Defense and the Just War," *World Futures*, 20, nos. 3/4 (1985): 151-178, and "Is the Principle of Double Effect Morally Acceptable?"

27. This and the following excerpt are from Khatchadourian, "Is the Principle?" 26.

28. Keenan, "Taking Aim," 203.

29. Lackey, *Ethics*, 60. Italics in original.

30. Ibid. Second Protocol (1977) of the Geneva Convention IV.

31. Lackey notes (p. 66) that the distinction "between death as a means or end and death as a side-effect, is not a distinction recognized in the ordinary [American] criminal law." Cf. Anscombe, "War and Murder," 46, concerning English law. Apart from the reasons I have given, a likely reason for the law's nonrecognition of that distinction is the difficulty of ascertaining the defendant's subjective intention as a putative mental disposition. That is, as it exists apart from the actual unlawful act of which the defendant is accused.

32. Fr. John C. Ford, "The Morality," in Wasserstrom, *War and Morality*, 38.

33. In considering the distinction between killing and letting die, in "Rights, Goals, and Fairness," (in *Consequentialism and Its Critics*, Samuel Scheffler, ed. [Oxford, 1991], 91), T. M. Scanlon states: "Opponents of the law of double effect have sometimes objected that it is

strange to make the permissibility of an action depend on quite subtle features of its rationale."

If the criticism is intended to mean that the principle of double effect's distinction between the unintended though knowing or foreseen killing of innocent persons and the intended killing of innocent persons is counterintuitive, the criticism may have a point. Understood in that way, my view that the distinction is morally irrelevant can be taken as saying that it is counterintuitive and hence, to that extent, morally unacceptable or at least not well founded.

Chapter 4

The Morality of Terrorism

II

In attempting to assess the morality of terrorism, in Chapter 2 I concentrated on arguments based on the relevant rules or conditions of just war theory and on human rights. In this chapter I shall continue that evaluation by focusing on consequentialist—specifically utilitarian—considerations designed to ascertain whether, first, an act-utilitarian, and second, a rule-utilitarian justification of some or all types or forms of terrorism may be forthcoming.[1] There are a number of specific reasons for this undertaking, in relation both to utilitarianism[2] and to so-called moderate deontologism, which applies various nonconsequentialist side-constraints to consequentialism, such as the protective norms of human rights and/or deontological principles of fairness and justice. In relation to both, it is necessary to examine the morality of terrorism. In the case of utilitarianism it is necessary because utilitarianism would reject the appeal I made in Chapter 2 to human rights and to nonconsequentialist principles of justice. Utilitarianism would also reject the princple of innocent immunity in relation to just war theory, if it is conceived as an absolute principle.[3] Consequently, it would dismiss as far from proven the overall conclusion I reached in Chapter 2, that terrorism in general, in all its various types and forms, is morally wrong. For, the general utilitarian position is that, theoretically speaking, some individual acts of terrorism or some type(s) or form(s) of terrorism are morally justifiable. And, some utilitarians maintain that some acts or forms of terrorism may also be justified in practice. Moreover, some hold that certain sorts of terrorism perpetrated during the past decades *have been* morally right, and that similar kinds of terrorist acts, under similar conditions, would also be right.

Moderate deontologism, insofar as it appeals to outcomes in judging the morality of actions, would also remain unconvinced by the arguments and conclusions in Chapter 2. In either case we must therefore try to ascertain whether these positions have any likelihood of being true.

Act-Utilitarianism and the Morality of Terrorism

I shall begin by granting that it is *theoretically* possible for individual acts of terrorism, in possible circumstances, to have good consequences on the whole. I shall go as far as to grant that it is possible for individual acts of terrorism, in certain theoretically possible circumstances, to have the best possible consequences in the circumstances. In granting the latter I am granting that, on general act-utilitarian grounds, it is theoretically possible for individual acts of terrorism to be morally right. I shall ignore the complex and difficult problems a utilitarian faces in trying to assess the relative degrees or extents of the goodness or badness of possible outcomes.

Having granted these things I turn to the question whether terrorist acts can, in practice, produce the greatest net good possible in the circumstances; indeed, whether they can even satisfy the less stringent condition of being actually good on the whole, rather than maximally good.

I think it is clear that the best or most promising candidates for an affirmative answer to this question would be acts of political or moralistic/religious terrorism "from below"; certainly not acts of predatory or retaliatory terrorism, or terrorism "from above." One would therefore expect that in trying to make the case the act-utilitarian would focus on the former. To see the truth of this I shall first consider the morality of predatory and retaliatory terrorism on general consequentialist grounds. If these types of terrorism are found to be indefensible on these general grounds, they would be a fortiori unjustifiable on act-utilitarian grounds.

Predatory and Retaliatiory Terrrorism

That no acts of predatory or retaliatory terrorism can be right on the strength of their overall outcomes is readily seen. No such acts perpetrated during the past several decades have resulted in anything like overall good consequences, let alone the best possible consequences in the circumstances. If that is any indication, it is very unlikely that future cases would be importantly different. Further, retaliatory terrorism is purely negative, reactive, a response to some real or imagined evil assumed to have been visited on individual terrorists, their organization, compatriots, or people. It lacks a positive objective and may or may not figure in the long-range goals of po-litical-moralistic/religious terrorism, or a national-liberationist revolutionary movement. Hostage-taking; exploding bombs at airports, plants, buildings, or other crowded places; and other forms of retaliation invariably backfire on the perpetrators and their organizations and supporters. They provoke either antiterrorism (judicial responses, retribution) or counterter-rorist (i.e., military) retaliation, or both. In the case of Pales-tinian terrorism directed against Israel during the past decades, we have witnessed a seemingly endless round of retaliations, counter-retaliations, counter-counter-retaliations, and so on.

Admittedly, retaliatory terrorism involving hostage-taking can be effective from the terrorists' point of view. As events in 1986 showed, hostage-taking may enable terrorists to extract considerable concessions from the targeted countries. The Reagan administration's attempts to swap arms for hostages, and the release of suspected or jailed terrorists in exchange for the release of hostages, are examples that come readily to mind. (On the other hand, consider those instances in which Western states have steadfastly refused to negotiate with ter-rorists for the release of hostages; or, as in Kuwait's case, to bow to terrrorist threats and acts of retaliation designed to force the government to release jailed terrorists.)

In no actual case I know of, however, have the terrorists' *ultimate* goals appreciably advanced by threats of retaliation or by actual retaliation. On the contrary, threats and acts of retaliation have led to the hardening of world opinion against any negotiations with terrorists or with states that support them—something likely to be repeated in the future. Again, another likely reason for the failure of retaliatory terrorism is stepped-up counterterrorism, including massive retaliation by the targeted governments.

Revolutionary Terrorism

In "Violence and Terorism: Its Uses and Abuses,"[4] Kai Nielsen presents a spirited defense of what he calls "revolutionary terrorism," which is a species of political terrorism and may be a species of moralistic/religious terrorism as well. His general thesis is that "we cannot, unless we can make the case for pacifism, . . ."[5] categorically rule out in all circumstances its [terrorism's] justifiable use even in what are formally and procedurally speaking democracies."[6]

The two kinds of "revolutionary violence" Nielsen defends are: "(1) revolutionary violence—the violence necessary to overthrow the state and to bring into being a new and better or at least putatively better social order—and (2) violence within a state when revolution is not an end but violence is only used as a key instrument of social change within a social system that as a whole is accepted as legitimate."[7] Nielsen adds: "it is often argued that, in the latter type of circumstances, a resort to violence is *never* justified when the state in question is a democracy."[8]

Nielsen's "revolutionary violence" logically includes (1') "revolutionary terrorism," defined by parity as "terrorism deemed necessary by the terrorists to overthrow the state and to bring a new and better or at least putatively better social order." His "violence within the state" includes (2') "terrorism within a state where terrorism is used as a key instrument of putative desirable social change within a social system that as a whole is accepted as legitimate."[9]

I shall begin, as he does, with Nielsen's second kind of socialist revolutionary terrorism. It is noteworthy that he limits himself to the attempt to justify individual acts of terrorism of that kind rather than the class of such acts; that is, he adopts an act-utilitarian criterion of right and wrong action.

The two conditions which, according to him, justified acts of revolutionary violence satisfy, are (1) that the revolutionaries "had good reason to believe" that their violent acts "might be effective," and (2) "they had good reason to believe that their . . . violence would not cause more injury and suffering all round than would simple submission or non-violent resistance to the violence directed against them by the state." His first example is of a democratically constituted government engaged in "institutional violence" against blacks in black ghettoes, whose rioting, occasioned by their long-standing condition, spill into white middle-class neighborhoods. The rioting causes the destruction of some property but not lives. The authorities respond by hauling blacks "to concentration camps (more mildly 'detention centers') for long periods of incarceration ('preventive detention') without attempting to distinguish the guilty from the innocent."[10] Nielsen thinks that blacks "would plainly be justified in resorting to violence to resist being so detained in such circumstances," if conditions (1) and (2) are satisfied.[11] My response to this is as follows.

Nielsen couches conditions (1) and (2) not in terms of the *actual* success of the blacks' putative moral purpose and the overall good's actually outweighing the injury and suffering caused by the counterviolence, but in terms of "good reasons," hence the *likelihood* of the preceding in terms of the facts available to the blacks at the time. As far as prospective action is concerned, Nielsen is right that "good reasons" are all that we can rationally go by. As Bertrand Russell somewhere says, probability is the guide to life, and,[12] clearly, rationality with respect to action consists in being guided by probabilities. Since the example assumes that blacks have good reasons for their expectations and hope that they will succeed, their action will be *rational*. But suppose the results turn out to be otherwise than expected: would their counterviolence be morally *right* on act-utilitarian grounds? Or would they be wrong although the agents themselves would not be morally blameworthy? Nielsen does not confront these crucial questions.[13]

Similar remarks apply to Nielsen's second and third examples: (2) Concerned citizens of a democratic superpower turning to violence, as a last resort, to disrupt "in some small measure" and "thus to weaken the 'institutional violence'" of their government as it wages "genocidal war of imeprialist aggression against a small, poor, underdeveloped nation."[14] (3)

The violence of a small ethnic minority in defense of its members' human rights, against their treatment as second-class citizens. It is unclear from Nielsen's description of example (2) whether the violence includes acts of terror, but (3) is clearly not an example of terrorism. In fact the same is true, mutatis mutandis, of example (1) considered earlier. In that example the blacks' use of force can be plainly viewed as an act of self-defence, not terrorism.[15] Further, Nielsen supposes—without evidence; indeed, erroneously—that whatever moral considerations apply to "revolutionary violence" in general, irrespective of the forms it takes, necessarily apply to "revolutionary terrorism" as well.

Rule-Utilitarianism and the Morality of Terrorism

National liberationist terrorism as part of a morally justified revolutionary movement constitutes the strongest case for the putative justifiability of terrorism on act-utilitarian grounds, not only in theory but also in practice. Nielsen's failure to provide convincing evidence for the latter dramatizes, a fortiori, the difficulties of justifying in practice acts of terrorism of any form or type on act-utilitarian grounds.

The difficulty in making a convincing case for the moral justifiability of any acts of terrorism in practice on act-utilitarian grounds pales beside the rule-utilitarian's difficulties. The rule-utilitarian encounters difficult theoretical problems, including problems concerning the rules that need to be formulated to that end.

Predatory and Retaliatory Terrorism and Rule-Utilitarianism

It can be readily seen that even if some individual *acts* of predatory or retaliatory terrorism satisfy the requirements of act-utilitarianism, the same would not be true of either of these two types of terrorism. It is difficult to imagine realistic situations in which predatory terrorism would be justifiable as a kind of act. Similarly, retaliatory terrorist acts as a class would be very unlikely to produce a net balance of good over evil. The morally-sanctioned general practice of acts of either type would almost certainy have dire overall consequences for any human society—would indeed tend to lead to a Hobbesian "state of nature" where fear, widespread distrust, and physical and psychological insecurity would make people's lives intolerable. The situation in Lebanon from 1975 until 1990 is a glaring example. If these conditions become widespread, they would dwarf the fear and uncertainty of travelers and others in large parts of the world.

Political-Moralistic Terrorism and Rule-Utilitarianism

A main theoretical difficulty that faces political-moralistic/ religious terrorism (such as the sort Kai Nielsen considers) is the problem of formulating rules which, if generally followed, would result in a net balance of good over evil. I mean rules having the form, "Acts of political-moralistic/religious terrorism with such-and-such characteristics: a, b, c, . . . ; or which is practised in such-and-such circumstances: C, D, E, . . . would result in a net balance of good over evil." For example: a rule that states that (1) terrorism is morally right if it forms part of a national-liberationist revolutionary movement: in general, terrorism that has a just cause. Or a rule that states that (2) in a formally and procedurally democratic state, terrorism by an oppressed minority targeted at the oppressing majority is right. In general terms, the desired rules would specify the sorts of terrorist acts that, in putatively favorable circumstances, would result in a net balance of good over evil. But whatever rules are proposed must make provision for the inescapable exceptions that would restrict their scope of application.

The unpredictability of future economic, social, political, military, and other relevant conditions in a changing world, particularly in certain parts of it, makes it impossible to build a fixed and exhaustive list of exceptions into the rule(s): conditions that would materially affect the outcomes of terrorist acts of various sorts.[16]

A prima facie possible way out would be for the rule-utilitarian to adopt the relevant rules of just war theory by adapting them to his position, that is, by thinking of them as nonabsolute, utilitarian rules. That means interpreting them—as all rule-utilitarian rules must be interpreted—as normative guidelines[17] to be retained (or retained without change) only so long as their general application continues to produce a net balance of good over evil. The question then becomes whether these rules, so understood, would serve to justify *any* form of terrorism. I shall return to this question.

It would seem that with the necessary modifications or restrictions, many of the conditions of just war theory can be adopted by the rule-utilitarian. The project is facilitated by the fact that (as I attempted to show in Chapter 3), a general consequentialist (but nonutilitarian) rationale can be provided for all the traditional principles of just war theory—including the principle of innocent immunity *if* it is reconceived as a nonabsolute rule of restricted scope. That is, they can be justified by the overall good consequences of their general adoption in various kinds of situations involving the use of force: war and civil war, revolution, coup d'etat, etc. This makes them prima facie natural candidates for adoption as utilitarian rules at least in relation to political-moralistic/religious terrorism.

Consequentialist Rationale for Just War Theory

The relevant conditions of just war theory here are: (1) right intention; (2) just cause; (3) proportionality as a political policy, in (a) O'Brien's and (b) Lackey's characterizations of it; (4) proportionality as a military principle; (5) necessity; (6) innocent immunity; (7) last resort and chance of success; and (8) just peace.

Right Intention, and Just Cause

The adoption of these conditions immediately restricts justifiable terrorism to the kind of case where the terrorism is in defense of the rights of the terrorists' country, community, or people, who are victims of oppression. The example Nielsen draws from twentieth-century African history applies here; in addition it may apply to Palestinian and Lebanese Shi'ite terrorism against Israel, and finally, perhaps, to IRA terrorism against Britain. A wide variety of types and forms of terrorism is excluded, most notably nondefensive state terrorism and predatory terrorism. Retaliatory terrorism against an oppressive state, community, or group strictly as part of collective self-defense may pass muster however.

Proportionality as a Political Policy

The adoption of this condition as characterized by O'Brien further restricts the theoretically justifiable forms of terrorism. As may be recalled from Chapter 2, O'Brien defines the political principle of proportionality as stipulating that the use of force must be "measured and restrained." Or adapting Donald Wells' formulation to the present situation, the harm inflicted on the oppressor must be proportional to the harm inflicted on the defender, the "righteous party." This theoretically eliminates, as a class, defensive terrorist policies and activities which inflict greater—especially considerably greater—harm on the oppressor than that inflicted on the terrorists and/or their oppressed community or people. The same would be true if the condition as characterized by Lackey is adopted. Adapting Lackey definition to terrorism, the conditions would stipulate that acts of terrorism "cannot be just unless the evil that can reasonably be expected to ensue from the [terrorism] is less than the evil that can reasonably be expected to ensue if the [terrorism] is not [practiced]."[19]

These proportionality conditions are complementary and so can be adopted together. Their adoption would however allow for *some* Palestinian terrorism directed strictly against Israel. But although some IRA terrorism against Britain may also be theoretically defensible on the first condition, it is difficult to say whether the same would be true on the second, because of the difficulty of assessing (certainly as far the prsent writer is concerned) the extent of the harms or evils endured by the Catholic minority in Northern Ireland under past and present British rule.

Proportionality as a "Military" Principle

This principle, in the form in which Lackey defines it, adapted to terrorism, stipulates that "the amount of destruction permitted in pursuit of a [specific terrorist] objective must be

proportional to the importance of the objective."[20] If adopted
it would impose further restrictions on the already much-re-
stricted theoretically defensible forms of terrorism.

Necessity, Last Resort,
Chance of Success, and Just Peace

The adoption of these conditions narrows down even further
the theoretically defensible forms of terrorism. In fact, if the
failure of all domestic and international political-moralistic/
religious movements during the past several decades is any
indication,[21] the adoption of the "chance of success" condition alone would eliminate in practice all political-moralistic/
religious terrorism that would still be defensible on the other
rules I have so far considered.[22]

Ironically the rule-utilitarian cannot avoid the "chance of
success" condition, even if he or she overtly excludes it. Whatever the type or form of terrorism they practice, success—especially ultimate success—is in every case the terrorists' objective. If the chances of success are practically nil, the terrorism
cannot be morally justified on general consequentialist
grounds. Practicing terrorism becomes utterly foolhardy and
irrational, suicidal, absurd.[23]

The rule-utilitarian does not fare much better if the "necessity" and "just peace" conditions are adopted. Although the
former can be overtly excluded from a set of rules, the utilitarian cannot avoid coming to terms with the latter condition; in
the same way that he or she cannot avoid confronting the
"chance of success" condition.

Lackey explains "the rule of just peace" in relation to war as
"a [*jus ad bellum*] rule that takes into consideration facts available to moral judges after the war ends. For war to be just, the
winning side must not only have obtained justice for itself: it
must not have achieved it at the price of violating the rights of
others. A just war must lead to a just peace."[24]

He observes that

> changes in international arrangements resulting from successful wars
> fought in self-defense may involve thousands of persons who were not
> parties to the conflict. It is in the interest of these victims of interna-
> tional upheavals that the rule of just outcome be applied. Such acts as

go beyond the restoration of the status quo ante, acts that provide
the victor with improved security or assess damages against the loser,
must not violate the rights of the citizens of the losing nation or the
rights of third parties.[25]

This condition can be readily adapted to the outcomes of
revolutionary-liberationist terrorism and other sorts of politi-
cal-moralistic/religious terrorism with just cause, etc. In considering the overall outcome of these forms of terrorism, it
too must be addressed by our typical utilitarian either by adopt-
ing it as a rule or by taking it into account in some other way.
Either way, the condition must be satisfied for the terrorism
to be morally defensible. For that to be true at least two things
are necessary: (a) the terrorists must achieve success, must realize their (just) ultimate goals; and (b) their success must somehow lead to the restoration of the rights of the immediate victims and the victimized, as well as those who are also harmed
by the terrorism. To quote Lackey again, they "must not violate the rights of the citizens in the losing nation or the rights
of third parties." [26]

Since terrorism involves appeal to violence—often including killing or wounding and maiming, hostage-taking, and the
like—it obviously cannot satisfy that condition, even in theory.
For how can the moral rights of those whose lives have been
directly or indirectly shattered, including those who have for-
ever lost the companionship or their loved ones to terrorist
violence, be ever restored?

I turn finally to "innocent immunity"; the "chance of success" condition will be discussed in relation to it.

Innocent Immunity

It will be recalled from Chapter 2 that terrorism in general
runs afoul of the absolute, unrestricted principle of innocent
immunity. Although it does allow for certain special exceptions in the form in which I maintain it, no act of terrorism of
any kind can possibly fall under any of these exceptions. For
in order that any deliberate or knowing terrorist act of killing
of an innocent person may *not* be murder, it must be performed
with the full knowledge or understanding and full consent of
the person to be killed! Indeed, the person must want to die—

if not also want to die at the hands of a person or persons he
or she requests or designates. (These are among the fundamental conditions for what I believe is morally justified active
or passive euthanasia, suicide, and assisted suicide. I leave aside
here the special case of nonvoluntary passive or active euthanasia.) Clearly, these conditions cannot possibly obtain in relation to terrorist killing of innocent persons. There is a veritable moral chasm between a terrorist's killing of an innocent
person and, for example, a physician's or a family member's
compassionately and lovingly performing euthanasia or assist-
ing in the voluntary suicide of a terminal cancer or AIDs patient suffering unbearable pain and mental anguish, who requests that his or her life be terminated.

The above-mentioned exceptions to the principle of innocent immunity are based on the right to individual freedom or
self-determination. Consequently, the rule-utilitarian who
wishes to adopt it in relation to (just cause, etc.) terrorism must
be able to provide convincing evidence that deliberately or
knowingly turning an innocent person into a victim, for the
sake of the terrorist's own projects and purposes, is morally
justified not only in theory but in practice under very special
conditions. Can such reasons be found? A possible answer is
given by Gerry Wallace in "Area Bombing, Terrorism and the
Death of Innocents,"[27] in relation to both war and terrorism,
in response to A.J. Coady's view in "The Morality of Terrorism."[28] In Wallace's words, Coady argues that

> terrorist acts, inasmuch as they involve the deliberate killing of inno-
> cent people, are morally indefensible. Terrorist campaigns even when
> they are in support of a "just" revolution, must conform to the rules
> governing what is permissible in a just war. And since targeting inno-
> cent people in a just war is unjustifiable, terrorist acts which do this
> are indefensible.[29]

Wallace rejects Coady's "absolutist approach to the killing
of innocent people"[30], which he calls "Internalism." He argues
that "in certain circumstances there are equally powerful and
accessible intuitions which support the opposite view."[31]

Although he takes "a rather different route" from such
consequentialists (utilitarians) as R.M. Hare and Richard
Brandt, Wallace reaches the same conclusion as they do in

what he describes as their rejection of "such intuitions both on general philosophical grounds and as adequate guides in war and other conflict situations."[32] He maintains that the counterintuitions to the Internalist case he provides "are perfectly compatible with various forms of consequentialism and could be justified along consequentialist lines."[33]

I shall not go into Wallace's criticism of the Internalist arguments he considers, with much of which I agree. I shall only concentrate on his positive claim that "although modern war does not obviate the distinction betwen innocent and noninnocent, it may sometimes be impossible to fight such wars *without, as it were, putting the distinction on one side*, and that it is sometimes permissible to do this."[34] I shall then consider whether his thesis, supposing it to be true, applies to terrorism.

Wallace's fundamental reason for his claim is essentially that in the case of war we must take account of "the situation of those countries or states or communities which are victims of unjustified attacks. Are we to say that their involvement in modern war, in their own defence, cannot be justified?"[35] The example on which he focuses is the daytime British area bombing of German cities in 1941, which (like the German area bombing of British cities) resulted in numerous civilian casualties. His reasoning there is essentially that Britain (1) was a victim of German aggression, and (2) was in mortal danger of invasion and loss of sovereignty and independence. Moreover, that British area bombing (3) was an absolutely last resort: the only hope of reversing the fortunes of a war that Britain was in grave danger of losing. Although he does not spell them out, it is clear that the "counter-intuitions" Wallace appeals to in relation to 1-3 are precisely the just war conditions of "just cause" (and "right intention"), "chance of success," and "last resort," respectively.

Wallace does not explicitly apply the foregoing considerations to terrorism, but assumes that they can serve to justify (mutatis mutandis) certain terrorist acts involving the deliberate killing of innocent persons.[36] If we adapt conditions 1-3 to terrorism, we get the following necessary conditions for "setting to one side" (or if you like, restricting) the absolute principle of innocent immunity. First, the country, people or community to which the terrorists belong must be a victim of aggression or oppression and must be defending itself either by terrorism alone or by terrorism as part of a popular uprising or revolution. That is, it must have just cause (1'). Second, the terrorism must be a last resort (2'); and third, it must present the victim country, people or community, etc., the last and so the only chance of success (3'). Note, however, that Wallace agrees with the Internalist that "there would appear to be some actions which no matter how good their consequences, we would not require anyone to do."[37] For instance (borrowing an example from Alan Gewirth) a man having to torture his mother to death in order to avert a terrorist missile attack on a city.[38]

I shall assume here, for the sake of argument, the correctness of restricting the principle of innocent immunity where the above conditions, 1'-3' obtain. The question I shall address is whether the rule-utilitarian's putative adoption of the principle of innocent immunity *with* the restrictions imposed on it by conditions 1'-3' would enable him to justify any acts of terrorism at all, in theory but especially in practice.

Our earlier discussion of these rules provides a quick answer to the question, since conditions 1'-3' are among those our rule-utilitarian is imagined to have already adopted. It is seen that the acceptance of the restricted principle of innocent immunity would severely hamper rather than advance the cause of the rule-utilitarian here. Although it would not theoretically rule out all terrorism without exception, its practical result would be precisely that. It is difficult to imagine any realistic situations in the present-day world or in the foreseeable future in which terrorism could be *either* (a) a last-resort defense, *or* (b) provide a victim country, people or community with the one and only chance of success against aggression or oppression—*a fortiori*, situations in which both (a) and (b) obtain. In fact, the implementation of condition (b) would sharply conflict with the political and "military" principles of proportionality which, in our earlier account, are already part of the adopted rules.

Again, it is difficult to see how the low-grade violence of terrorism rather than the highergrade forms of violence, such as (defensive) uprisings, rebellions and revolutions, and above all wars, can be a last resort in a victimized people's or country's struggle to remove, say, a foreign or indigenous yoke. For instance, it is no accident that Palestinian terrorism started decades before the intifada.[39] Although the latter was a grassroots movement in the occupied territories and was not started by the PLO, the PLO supported it as a more effective form of resistance, particularly in drawing the world's attention to the Palestinians' plight, once that organization came to perceive terrorism as an essentially passing (if not ultimately ineffectual) phase in the struggle against Israel.[40]

Terrorist activities taking place in the context of uprisings, revolutions, civil wars, or wars, including the kind of revolutionary-liberationist movement considered by Kai Nielsen, are no exception. Terrorism is and remains ancillary to much more forceful means of collective self-defense.

As for terrorism's chances of success, they tend to vary immensely with the strength of the targeted country's response in the form of antirevolutionary (nonmilitary) and, especially, counterrevolutionary (military) responses. These efforts to combat terrorism tend to gain in strength as the terrorism becomes bloodier and causes increasing military and civilian casualties. Consequently, a terrorist movement's chances of realizing its ultimate or even intermediate objectives become increasingly slim, although immediate goals, such as gaining notoriety, may be more than realized.

Gaining the world's moral and perhaps political sympathy for the justice of an assumed just cause through the violent dramatization of their grievances is of course a main immediate and intermediate objective of political-moralistic/religious terrorism. But the amount of that moral capital, if it ever materializes, tends to vary inversely with the degree and extensiveness of the violence perpetrated. To maximize their chances of gaining sympathy, the violence terrorists perpetrate must be minimal and confined. It must exclude indiscriminate mass killings of civilians (especially women and children) in crowded public places, kidnappings and hostage-taking—in short, acts that outrage public opinion. For instance, if hostages are taken, they must be released as soon as possible. From the terrorists' standpoint, the irony is of course that the less violent the terrorist acts, the easier it becomes for the world to ignore them as well as for the targeted governments to suppress them. In that case, too, success would elude the terrorists.

From the very start, one particularly important fact works against and tends to repel more than attract sympathy for terrorists of all stripes, including just-cause terrorists, and so makes the attainment of their ultimate goals even more problematic. That fact is the widespread conviction we encountered in Chapter 1, that terrorist killings are cold-blooded murder—if not that their perpetrators are irrational or even crazy as well.

The overall negative conclusion one can draw from the discussion so far about the justifiability of terrorism in relation to consequentialism in general and utilitarianism in particular, is, ultimately, not too dissimilar to R.M. Hare's (as a utilitarian) overall assessment of terrorism. In a private communication he wrote[41]:

> For myself, I would agree on utilitarian grounds that terrorism is practically always in practice wrong; one can conceive of situations in which [on act-utilitarian grounds] it would be right, but they occur so seldom, if at all, that it is optimific to inculcate the intuitive [rule-utilitarian] principle that it is always wrong.

Rule-Utilitarianism and Human Rights

Human rights—rights people have simply as human beings—are necessarily independent of any consequentialist, including utilitarian, moral principles. Consequently, no human-rights norms can be incorporated into a rule-utilitarian scheme by being subsumed as subordinate rules (as they must then be) under utilitarian or other consequentialist principles. That is, they cannot provide rules that are always open to being restricted or set aside whenever their implementation conflicts or is believed to conflict with the general welfare, however defined. I do not mean just in those extreme cases where the *exercise* of particular human rights of some individuals or groups of individuals may need to be overridden by greater and more pressing moral demands.[42] Thus even if (as I myself believe) human rights are not thought of as absolute protective norms, appeal to human rights would not serve the rule-utilitarian concerned to defend just-cause political-moralistic/religious terrorism.

But further, and as I argued in Chapter 2, appeal to human rights serves to condemn rather than to justify all types and forms of terrorism. Suppose that the rule-utilitarian tries to combine human-rights norms with the "right intention," "just cause," and "just peace" rules carried over from our earlier discussion. As we saw in Chapter 1, terrorists targeting *any* innocent or noninnocent individuals as a means of coercing some group or government whose behavior or policy they want to influence, would directly violate these individuals' right to be treated as persons. The same is true in relation to an individual's human right to be free to strive for self-fulfillment, or any right promulgated by the UN's Universal Declaration of Human Rights. The same can I think be shown to be true, mutatis mutandis, in relation to any other well-known theory of human rights.[43]

To sum up: Continuing the moral evaluation of terrorism, particularly political and moralistic/religious terrorism, begun in Chapter 2, this chapter inquired whether terrorism fares better, at least in certain circumstances, on consequentialist grounds: specifically, on act-utilitarianism (Kai Nielsen's) and on certain forms of rule-utilitarianism. The examination showed, however, that in practice terrorism is always morally unjustifiable, even on act-utilitarian grounds, where it makes the stronger case. Further support for our general conclusion regarding the morality of terrorism is to be found in the critical examination of Burleigh Taylor Wilkins' consequentialist defense of "terrorism" in certain circumstances, in the following appendix to this chapter.

In short, the critical examination of the morality of terrorism, as a whole, has led to one basic conclusion: that terrorism in general, in all its types and forms, is never morally justifiable but in fact is always morally wrong.

Appendix

In his book *Terrorism and Collective Responsbility*,[44] Burleigh Taylor Wilkins defends terrorism under "certain circumstances"; that is, terrorism as a putative "species of self-defense"[45] in the presence of "collective guilt toward which the terrorism is directed."[46] As the quotation indicates, Wilkins' defense essentially involves an appeal to the principle of collective self-defense, which he grounds on the natural right not to be injured or harmed, together with three fundamental moral principles of just war theory: the principle of last resort, the principle of innocent immunity, and the political and military principles of proportionality. He also appeals, like Nielsen, to act-consequentialist (utilitarian) arguments designed to show that, in a number of familiar historical cases, terrorism, as part of a national liberationist revolutionary movement, has helped to throw off the yoke of foreign domination (if not to usher in a better political, economic, or social order).

To justify terrorism as a putative species of *collective* self-defense, Wilkins utilizes the crucial concepts of collective moral responsibility, liability, and guilt: the collective guilt of those groups, communities, or institutions that are guilty of perpetrating great injury or harm on the terrorists themselves or on the group to which they belong, and so are the targets of terrorist violence as an instrument of self-defense.

In this appendix I concentrate on Wilkins' central arguments and attempt to show that they fail to provide convincing rational or factual evidence in support of his central thesis regarding terrorism, thus concluding the evaluation of the morality of terrorism in this book.

Wilkins on Sufficient Conditions for Justifiable Terrorism

In Chapter 1 of his book, Wilkins proposes a rule that provides what he considers to be a sufficient condition for justifiable terrorism. It states that "terrorism is justified as a form of self-defense when: (1) all political and legal remedies have been exhausted or are inapplicable (as in emergencies where 'time is of the essence'); (2) the terrorism will be directed against members of a community or group which is collectively guilty of violence aimed at those individuals who are now considering the use of terrorism as an instrument of self-defense, or at the community or group of which they are members."⁴⁷ To the rule he adds three constraints concerning its applications which I shall consider in the following discussion.

With relatively minor changes, the preceding rule together with the three added constraints provides an excellent albeit partial set of moral conditions or guidelines for the justifiability not of terrorism, as Wilkins thinks, but of forms of violence very different from terrorism—commonly called "freedom fighting"—which he confuses with or assimilates to terrorism. These are forms of violence which under certain conditions—that is, whenever they aim at collective freedom from domestic oppression or foreign domination or aggression, would include uprisings, rebellions and revolutions, coups d'etat, and war. Unlike terrorism, "freedom fighting" in all its forms is essentially "monofocal, and these forms of violence are, by definition, bona fide forms of collective self-defense against what is perceived to be domestic or foreign social, political, economic, religious, etc. injury or harm.

The source of Wilkins' inability to distinguish terrorism, or to distinguish it clearly and adequately, from other species of violence, is his seriously flawed definition of 'terrorism,' which is both too wide and too narrow. It is too wide as a result of failure to include the terrorism's essential "bifocal" feature, though he is abstractly aware of the existence of that feature in his acceptance of Carl Wellman's (not very apt) distinction between the "primary" and the "secondary" targets of terrorism.⁴⁸ According to the definition, terrorism is "the attempt to achieve political, social, economic, or religious change by the actual or threatened use of violence against persons or property." Worse still, although Wilkins recognizes that the definition is too broad, he is (strangely) unsure whether "on the level of definition terrorism can be distinguished from war and revolution."⁴⁹

In other "directions" the definition is also extremely narrow; since the only types of terrorism to which it applies are political and political-moralistic/religious terrorism; and among these it only applies to terrorism from below.[50] Nor are the addenda to the definition much help. Thus the first addendum—which, by the way, overemphasizes the publicizing of the terrorists' goals or cause at the expense of "destabilizing the existing political or social order[51]—fails to distinguish the immediate/intermediate (e.g., publicity) and the ultimate goals (e.g., political destabilization) of terrorist acts. The second addendum, which states that "often, though not always, terrorism is aimed at provoking extreme counter-measures which will help win public support for the terrorists and their cause,"[52] like the first addendum, applies only (and then quite problematically and at best only sometimes) to political-moralistic/religious terrorism from below. The final addendum, that "terrorism is . . . properly understood as an activity of not only the weak but the desperate,"[53] is only true of terrorism from below—and at the same time also true of some uprisings, rebellions, and coups d'etat, and even wars and revolutions, and so does not help to distinguish terrorism from them.

As stated above, the basic reason terrorism cannot be a species of self-defense under any circumstances is its bifocal character and the monofocal character of collective as well as individual self-defense. This can be clearly seen, for example, by considering the difference between Wilkins' hypothetical case of Jewish terrorism against the Nazi holocaust and the use of violence in bona fide collective self-defense, as in the case of the Jewish Warsaw Ghetto uprising. Although both would have had similar goals—ultimately, to help stop Hitler from persecuting and killing Jews—the means or methods used to achieve them would have been significantly different. In the Warsaw uprising the Jews fought directly against Nazi soldiers in order to prevent being sent to a Nazi labor camp—and to death. They did not (as they would have done had they practiced terrorism) attempt to kidnap or assassinate, say, some Nazi diplomat or high-placed government official—Goebbels or Goring, for example, or a Nazi general—or bomb the Reichstag, to force Hitler to stop the persecution of the Jews.

The same difference can be seen if we compare the attempt of the Reichstag conspirators to assassinate Hitler in the hope of ending the Second World War, with the hypothetical terrorist assassination in my preceding example. The former's monofocal character in contrast to the latter's bifocal character should be evident.

The difference I am trying to emphasize can be clearly illustrated by considering individual self-defense, which involves the same basic pattern in question as collective self-defense. If someone attacks me, I can be properly said to be defending myself only if I attempt to prevent the attacker from harming me. I cannot be properly said to be defending myself if, instead of using force directly against him or her I use force against anyone else who is not attacking me, even if he or she is standing there inciting or abetting the attacker but not actually physically attacking me, protecting the attacker, or otherwise physically preventing me from defending myself against the attacker. On the other hand I would be committing a terrorist act if I used force against the inciter, abetter, or protector as a way of forcing my attacker to desist.

Essentially the same problem with Wilkins' position is seen in relation to the logical conflict between terrorism's bifocal nature and the perfectly rational and, in themselves, perfectly moral demands of two of the three moral constraints Wilkins places on terrorism in the application of his general rule. The second constraint stipulates that "as far as possible terrorism should be confined to 'primary targets,' and where that is not possible the terrorist should pick a 'secondary target' who is as guilty or nearly as guilty, in the sense of being responsible for initiating or participating in the violence which can be said to have 'started it all' and which is continuing."[54] The third constraint stipulates that "the terrorism in question should be directed initially at the perpetrators of violence and then at their accomplices in such a way as to reflect the part they played in the violence. If the terrorism still fails to achieve its goal, the successful defense of the terrorists or the community . . . they [the terrorists] should proceed to violence against those who, as individuals, are guilty of moral complicity in the violence in question."[55] In terms of Wilkins' four categories of collectively guilty individuals—"perpetrators," "abetters," "inciters," and "protectors"—the constraints enjoin the terrorist to direct his violence first (and if successful, last as well) at the perpetrators, rather than at the less responsible and conse-

quently less guilty "abetters" and "inciters," or the still less
guilty "protectors."

As I have said, these constraints are both rational and, as
such, perfectly moral. They are rational since they are intended
to enable the terrorists to achieve the ultimate goal envisaged
by Wilkins: ending the violence against them and the group to
which they belong. For supposing certain favorable conditions
to be present, the direct targeting of the perpetrators (foremost among whom would be the planners or masterminds of
the violence against the terrorists) would have the greatest
chance of success. The constraints are also moral since, like
Wilkins, we are here concerned with social-political/moralis-
tic terrorism that has a just cause, not with retaliatory terrorism, which aims at revenge.

Once again and for reasons quite similar to those which ren-
der self-defense incompatible with the bifocal character of terrorism discussed earlier, these constraints are incompatible
with that same feature of terrorism.

Collective Guilt and Innocent Immunity

As stressed in Chapter 4 and in Chapter 2, innocent immunity
is an absolutely fundamental condition of the justifiability of
any use of force or violence.[56] But no attempt to apply that
priniple to the question of collective guilt, and so to a defense
of terrorist violence, can get off the ground unless a clear,
defensible account of the murky concept of collective guilt is
forthcoming. But that is precisely what we do not find in the
pages of Wilkins's book. Time and again Wilkins' attempts to
elucidate that concept fail. In particular, they fail to provide
clear guidelines or criteria for collective guilt and so for drawing even hazy boundaries around the concept. For instance, it
is anything but clear what classes of people are, in general,
excluded from collective responsibility; i.e., are to be counted
as innocent, hence exempt from justifiable terrorist attacks.
What we are explicitly offered as non-innocents are four very
general and vague groups of individuals: perpetrators, abetters, inciters, and protectors, and just two categories of innocents : those who are unwillfully ignorant of the collective evils
perpetrated, and where membership is not voluntary.[57] In fact

Wilkins casts the net of collective guilt much too widely by
defining the collectively guilty as all those who stand to benefit from membership in the guilty group. He says: "It is in
their interest to belong, or else they would not, though of course
this assumes that membership is voluntary."[58] In saying this he
ignores the obvious logical fact that although all those who
are guilty (presumably) stand to benefit from membership in
the group, the converse neither logically follows nor is always
actually true.

Finally, in Chapter 3, "Terrorism and Consequentialism,"
Wilkins offers several actual examples from the recent past
designed to demonstrate that, as part of a national revolutionary movement, terrorist activities can help bring about a better social order. For he admits that by itself terrorism has not
so far succeeded in bringing about liberation from a bad order or brought about a better new order.

The examples he uses (which, by the way, do not or did not
all involve terrorism as part of a revolution) are Kenyan and
Jewish terrorism against British colonial rule in Kenya and
Palestine respectively, the assassination of Archduke Ferdinand
by a Serbian nationalist, which triggered World War I, and the
Provisional IRA terrorism in Northern Ireland. In the case of
the first example and in all other cases where terrorism has
been part of a revolution, coup d etat, or war, Wilkins encounters the same problems we saw in Chapter 4 in relation to Kai
Nielsen s similar claims; that is, the impossibility of knowing,
hence the unavailability of factual evidence regarding the actual positive contribution of the terrorism (if anything) to the
revolution, etc. as a whole, and consequently, whether the revolution would or could have succeeded in the absence of terrorism. Not surprisingly, Wilkins makes no effort to provide such
evidence. Worse still, he creates an insoluble conceptual problem for himself in relation to these and other possible examples
by his earlier declaration in the book that he is not sure that
on the level of definition [whatever that means] terrorism can
be distinguished from war and revolution.[59] And nowhere else
does he tell us how, on some other (presumably practical) level
terrorism, revolution, and war can be distinguished.

In fact, whatever the contribution of Mau Mau terrorism in
Kenya to Kenyan independence, Jewish terrorism (and Pales-

tinian violence) in Palestine was in my view not a major factor in Britain s decision to pull out of Palestine and hand the very complicated Palestine Problem to the United Nations (see the Appendix at the end of this book). As for the assassination of Archduke Ferdinand, it is obvious that the liberation of Serbia from the Austro-Hungarian Empire resulted not from the assassination itself (as Wilkins strangely alleges) but from the war it triggered—which after four years of bloodshed (for which the great European powers were long preparing), ended in, among other things, the Austro-Hungarian Empire's demise.[60] This, apart from the moot question of whether the assassination was a terrorist act or a straightforward nonterrorist act of political assassination. Finally, as far as IRA terrorism is concerned, the jury is still out.

Notes

1. The present discussion is limited to the simplest forms of utilitarianism. But I think it can be shown that, with the necessary modifications, the discussion and my conclusions would apply to more complex and cophisticated forms, such as those of R. M. Hare and Richard Brandt.

2. For the purpose of this chapter and the book as a whole, I shall ignore the many often valid criticisms leveled at contemporary as well as classical utilitarianism. See, for example: Bernard Williams, with J. J. C. Smart, *Utilitarianism, For and Against* (Cambridge, 1973)); Bernard Williams, *Ethics and the Limits of Philosophy* (Cambridge, MA, 1985); and John Rawls, *A Theory of Justice* (Cambridge, MA, 1971). A few other relevant writings include: Bernard Williams and Amartya Sen, eds., *Utilitarianism and Beyond* (Cambridge, 1982); and Samuel Scheffler, ed., *Consequentialism and Its Critics* (Oxford, 1991).

3. I specify "absolute" since, as we shall seed in Chapter 6, the various conditions of just war theory except an absolute principle of innocent immunity can be given a consequentialist if not utilitarian justification, provided that they are not conceived of as absolute, exceptionless rules.

4. Kai Nielsen, "Violence and Terrorism, Its Uses and Abuses," in Burton M. Leiser, *Values in Conflict* (New York, 1981), 435-449.

5. If my claims concerning the existence of human rights in general and the right to be treated as a moral person in particular are essentially correct, Nielsen is mistaken in claiming that only by making the case for pacifism can the moral justifiability of terrorism in all circumstances be ruled out. For a consideration of some of the main difficulties in universal pacifism, see Haig Khatchadourian, "Pacifism," *World Futures*, 21, nos. 3/4 (1985): 263-278.

6. Nielsen, "Violence and Terrorism," 435.

7. Ibid., 438.

8. Ibid. Italics in original.

9. Ibid. Nielsen describes terrorism in the context of a social revolutionary activity as follows (p. 445): "In this context we should view terrorism as a tactical weapon in achieving a socialist revolution. . . . A terrorist is one who attempts to further his or her political ends by means of coercive intimidation, and terrorism is a systematic policy designed to achieve that end."

10.   Nielsen, "Violence and Terrorism," 438.

11.   Ibid.

12.   In a private communication to the author, Professor Antony Flew stated that if Bertrand Russell said that, he was "presumably, quoting the good Joseph Butler who ended Section 4 of the Introduction to his *Analogy of Religion* with the words: 'To us, probability is the very guide to life.'"

13.   In opposition to Kai Nielsen's position, Bernard Williams, in "A Critique of Utilitarianism," argues that for direct (i.e., act-) utilitarianism "right action" is an objective maximizing notion, distinguishable from a rational action; that is, it "is not bounded by the agent's state of knowledge at the time, and the claim that he did the wrong thing is compatible with recognizing that he did as well as anyone in his state of knowledge could have done." (Williams, *Utilitarianism, For and Against*, 86).

One possible way of dealing with the preceding is to distinguish between "subjective rightness" and "objective rightness," identifying the former with a rational but nonoptimific action. An objectively right action would then be an action that actually maximizes the good. In any event, if an action is rational (or "subjectively right") the *agent* himself cannot be justly blamed if his action fails to maximize the good.

14.   Nielsen, "Violence and Terrorism," 439.

15.   Self-defense, whether individual or collective, is logically different from terrorism. For one thing, this is so because it lacks the "bifocal" character of terrorism. It consists in the use of physical force against an attacker or aggressor to prevent or minimize harm to oneself and/or one's group, people, country, etc. But terrorism may sometimes aim at the defense or protection of a group, a country, or a people as an ultimate objective.

16.   This situation, which faces rule-utilitarianism across the entire spectrum of possible moral situations, leads to one of the important criticisms of this type of theory by act-utilitarians as well as nonutilitarians. I refer to what J. J. C. Smart, following David Lyons, speaks of as the danger of the rule-utilitarian's "rule-worship." But it can be shown that it is an error to think, as Lyons and Smart do, that the avoidance of that danger would (logically speaking) reduce rule-utilitarianism to act-utilitarianism.

This erroneous criticism must not be confused with the related but valid point that a rule-utilitarian would not be a consistent utilitarian if he or she does not allow individual exceptions to the rules even when following them has a counterutilitarian outcome.

17.   Essentially, as inductive generalizations based on past and present experience, but reconceived as normative, moral rules within a rule-utilitarian scheme.

18.   Douglas Lackey, *The Ethics of War and Peace* (Englewood Cliffs, NJ, 1989), 40.

19.   Ibid.

20.   Ibid., 59.

21.   That is, distinguishing the success or failure of the terrorism as such from the success or failure of revolutionary movements that may have included terrorism.

22.   It is conceivable that conditions may change so drastically in the future that some terrorist movements may succeed. One such (horrifying) possibility pertains to nuclear terrorism; that is, a terrorist group acquiring a nuclear bomb and using it to coerce and intimidate a country or group of countries to accede to its demands. As long as that is (or remains) only a remote posssibility, the point made in the text remains. Nonetheless, the nightmare of nuclear terrorism underlines the responsibility of the entire world community to take all necessary prcautions to prevent such a doomsday scenario from becoming a reality.

23.   Lackey, *Ethics*, 41-42, faults the Finns for resisting the Russian invasion of their country in 1939, despite the justice of their cause. He criticizes them for resisting against manifestly overwhelming odds, and so, violating the military principle of proportionality.

24.   Ibid., 43.

25.   Ibid., 43-44. The creation of non-fly zones by the UN and the USA in northern and southern Iraq (and more recently another zone south of Baghdad), and the imposition of other restrictions on Saddam Hussein's government with regard to the Kurds in the north and the Shi'ite Muslims in the south, are good examples of this in the aftermath of the Persian Gulf War.

26.   Ibid., 44.

27.   Gerry Wallace, "Area Bombing, Terrorism and the Death of Innocents," in *Applied Philosophy: Morals and Metaphysics in Contemporary Debate*, Brenda Almond and Donald Hill, eds. (London, 1991), 128-140.

28.   A. J. Coady, "The Morality of Terrorism," in *Philosophy* (1985), 47-69.

29.   Wallace, "Area Bombing," 128.

30.   Ibid., 129.

31. Brenda Almond and Donald Hill, summarizing Wallace's central claim, *Applied Philosophy*, 128.

32. Ibid., 129.

33. Ibid.

34. Ibid., 132. Italics added.

35. Ibid.

36. We need to add "deliberate" (if not also "or knowing") not only because deliberateness is an essential part of the Roman Catholic principle of innocent immunity, but also—and more particularly here—because that is what the analogy with British area bombing requires. It is a historical fact that the killing of German civilians (just as in the case of German area bombing of British cities) was intended to demoralize the German people, in addition to destroying whatever military centers and the like that were located in the cities bombed.

37. Alan Gewirth, "Are There Any Absolute Rights?" *Philosophical Quarterly*, 31, 1-16, cited in *Applied Philosophy: Morals and Metaphysics in Contemporary Debate*, Brenda Almond and Donald Hill, eds. (London, 1991), 136.

38. Ibid.

39. Since Yasser Arafat's renouncing terrorism, there have been a few but no major PLO or PLO-supported acts of terrorism.

40. Paul Saba, in his "The Armenian National Question," in *Power and Stability in the Middle East*, Berch Berberoglu, ed. (London, 1989), 197, states that Yasser Arafat's victory at the 19th Palestinian National Council in Algeria in 1988 was "primarily a result of the intifada in the occupied territories and new diplomatic openings for the PLO in the West which dramatically demonstrated the soundness of the strategy proposed by the Fateh majority and its allies [against the Fateh minority and pro-Syrian forces of the 'National Bloc,' who would subordinate the Palestinian struggle to Syrian national interests and a narrowly military strategy]."

41. Letter to the author, 6 January 1989. Hare adds, referring to my arguments in "Terrorism and Morality" (reprinted with some additions in chapters 1 and 2 of this book): "I shall therefore not find myself in accord with what I take to be your line of reasoning [I assume, my appeal to just war theory and, especially, human rights], though I also disagree with Kai Nielsen, so far as I remember his arguments in a symposium in which we took part a long time ago." Hare's reference is to "*On Terrorism, Journal of Value Inquiry*," v. 13 (1979). Reprinted in his *Essays on Political Morality* (Oxford, 1989).

42. I have in mind such catastrophic circumstances as the threat to the survival of an entire people or the human race, the entire physical world, or all living things on earth.

43. A last-ditch effort to justify terrorism would be to claim that terrorist acts are amoral, in the sense that they are neither right nor wrong—that moral categories do not apply to them. This claim would lack plausibility except in the case of international terrorism from above, since the latter would fall under the general view known as "moral realism." On that view, in contrast to "political moralism," moral assessments are useless and inapplicable to relations between states.

44. Burleigh Taylor Wilkins, *Terrorism and Collective Responsibility* (London and New York, 1992).

45. Ibid., 31.

46. Ibid., 29. There Wilkins also states that "perhaps rationales for terrorism which do not depend upon whether self-defense is involved might be constructed, but I shall not explore the possibility here, nor shall I consider whether terrorism in the absence of any collective guilt toward which the terrorism is directed might somehow be justified."

47. Ibid., 28.

48. Although the "victimized" are the "primary" (in the sense of the "real" or "ultimate" albeit "indirect") target of terrorism, it is misleading to call the "immediate victims" of terrorism the "secondary" targets rather than, say, "immediate" or "direct" targets. But no matter.

49. Both quotes: Wilkins, 2-3.

50. Although in Chapter 1 he speaks of the Nazi holocaust of the Jews as terrorism by characteristically confusing genocide with or assimilating it to terrorism!

51. Wilkins, 3.

52. Ibid.

53. Ibid., 4.

54. Ibid., 29.

55. Ibid., 30.

56. I leave aside the practical fact (important for consequentialist attempts to defend terrorism) that, in the case of terrorism, abiding by the principle of innocent immunity is much easier said than done.

57. Wilkins, 139.

58. Ibid., 138-139. Note for instance that in Chapter 1 he says that all Germans were guilty of the holocaust against the Jews, and in Chapter 7 (p. 145), that in the case of organized groups such as nation states, "*all* the individual members of the collective . . . may be considered vicariously responsible for the wrongful actions done by that collective." (Italics added.) Earlier (p. 138) he says that "vicarious liability" arises "when a representative of a group, acting as such . . .

has committed a harmful act; ascriptions of vicarious liability to a group are justifiable when the harmful act in question is also a rights violation."

59. Ibid., 2-3.

60. Cf. "World War I," *Collier's Encyclopedia*, 1991, v. 23: "In the Balkans, the several states lived normally, so it seemed, in a state of crisis, and looking over their heads were the towering shadows of Teutonic Pan-Germanism in conflict with Russian Pan-Slavism."

Chapter 5

"Freedom Fighting": Nature and Morality

In preceding chapters I have noted that during the past several decades the word "terrorism" has been often deployed as a psychological-political weapon, a loose, blanket term for all sorts of violenct acts directed against communities, governments, or countries by individuals or groups with, for example, some real or imagined grievance against their targets, not only for bona fide terrorism as understood in Chapter 1. An extreme example was Mr. Rabin's calling the "stone children" of the Palestinian intifada "terrorists." I also noted, in discussing the nature of terrorism in Chapter 1, that the targets of attacks naturally consider their attackers to be terrorists. On the other hand, the PLO leadership considered their own organization to consist of "freedom fighters," not terrorists. The same "them-us" duality arises in relation to the Lebanese Shi'ites who attack Israeli troops in Southern Lebanon. It may be recalled that some years ago President Hafez al-Asad, probably stung by the United States branding Syria as a terrorist state, called for an international conference to consider the nature of "freedom fighting" and so to differentiate it from terrorism.

The tendency to confuse terrorism and freedom fighting points to a practical as well as theoretical need for drawing a proper distinction between "terrorism" and "freedom fighting." Unfortunately, I find little interest on the part of scholars to demarcate the two concepts, or to make a careful examination of the concept or the general nature of "freedom fighting" itself. A better understanding of that concept and its difference from terrorism is also essential for its moral assessment, which is clearly germane to the proper response to "freedom fighting" by governments, international bodies, and world public opinion.

For these and related reasons, the present chapter will be devoted to an attempt to understand the nature and morality of "freedom fighting."

Definitions

"Freedom fighting" is an umbrella term. In the broad sense of "fighting," as a struggle, freedom fighting can be peaceful, as for example in the active nonviolent resistance practiced by Mahatma Gandhi and his followers, and by Martin Luther King, Jr., and his followers. Other nonviolent forms of freedom fighting are strikes, demonstrations, sit-ins, and other forms of civil disobedience. However, because of the word "fighting," the term "freedom fighting" is usually understood in a more restricted sense to refer solely to an individual's or, more commonly, a group's or a people's armed struggle against oppressive indigenous rule or foreign domination—indicated by the word "freedom."

"Freedom fighting," in the broad use of the term, is a "range," and so, an open concept. It covers a wide variety of activities which (a) paradigmatically include engaging in a rebellion or a guerilla war of national liberation, such as the very recent armed struggle of the Chechnyans for independence from Russia. It also includes (b) sporadic fighting by small, irregular urban or rural bands of fighters. The Shi'ite bands—as opposed to Hizbollah, the Party of God—that occasionally ambush small Israeli forces or fight the Israeli-equipped Christian militia in South Lebanon, are another example. "Freedom fighting" may also include (c) the sort of guerrilla warfare conducted by South African nationalists against the white South African government, in incursions from across the South African borders.

A necessary step in distinguishing terrorism and "freedom fighting" is to distinguish two concepts that are normally conjoined, namely "terrorism" and "acts of terrorism." Logically speaking, it is perfectly possible for the same individual or group to practice "freedom fighting" as well as to perform terrorist acts; but we can also meaningfully speak of a particular individual as more of a terrorist than a "freedom fighter," or the opposite. For the sake of simplicity I shall limit the word "terrorist" to individuals who habitually or exclusively indulge in terrorist acts, as these were described in Chapter 1. In that way an individual whose actions satisfy the definition of "freedom fighting" and only occasionally commits small-scale terrorist acts, inflicting little physical or mental harm on the immediate victims and the victimized, could be more appropriately called a "freedom fighter" than a "terrorist."

In this stipulated usage, then, a freedom fighter is, negatively speaking, an individual who in fighting against an *unjsut* or *evil* political ruler, system, or regime does not indulge in terrorist activities at all or only occasionally indulges in relatively small-scale acts of that kind. As we shall presently see, this proviso is essential, whether one understands "freedom fighting" to be morally justified by definition, as I think is usually the case, or whether, as I use the term, it is a value-neutral term and so may or may not be morally justifiable in general or in certain kinds of cases.

I mentioned the Chechnyans, black South African guerrillas, and South Lebanese Shi'ite fighters as paradigms of freedom fighters. The characteristics these and other paradigms of freedom fighting have in common, hence their essential difference from terrorism, are I think the following. First, the wholly and solely defensive purpose of freedom fighting, which is the struggle for collective freedom. Second, the avoidance of deliberate (if not also knowing) targeting of civilians (innocent persons), limiting itself as much as possible to attacks on the military forces it is combating. Third and most fundamentally, the absence of the "bifocal" character essential to terrorism. "Freedom fighting" does not resort to the coercion or intimidation of any individual or group, indulge in kidnappings, hostage-taking, torturing, maiming or killing in cold blood. In fact, "freedom fighters" typically do not take prisoners, perhaps partly because the hit-and-run guerrilla warfare they frequently resort to makes prisoner-taking impracticable or undesirable. Normally—that is, except when the fighters aim to capture a head of state in their drive for political freedoms—any prisoners captured are taken by happenstance, in the heat of battle, not deliberately as happens in political and moralistic terrorism. Even when prisoners are taken, they are not normally used as pawns to coerce the powers that be, and are released unharmed.

As stated earlier, freedom fighting may take the form of an uprising or rebellion, a coup d'etat, a civil war, or a war, each of which may be in the form of or include rural or urban guerrilla warfare. For example, revolutionaries (say waging a guerrilla war) may be freedom fighters, and freedom fighters may be revolutionaries. Leiser captures the essentials of guerilla warfare when he states that it is characterized by small-scale, unconventional, limited actions carried out by irregular forces *"against regular military forces, their supply lines, and communications."*[1] Many of the recent rebellions or civil wars in Latin America and in various parts of Africa have involved rural and sometimes urban guerrilla fighting. The Southern Lebanese Shi'ites fighting against Israeli military forces also illustrate rural guerrilla warfare. On the other hand, the Palestinian intifada was largely an urban phenomenon and did not involve any guerrilla fighting. Finally, European underground resistance movements against Nazi occupation are further examples of guerilla warfare, in that case during a genocidal war.

Freedom Fighting and Morality
In what follows I shall consider the conditions of morally justifiable freedom fighting by focusing on revolution as one major form (successful) "freedom fighting" may take. I shall leave it to the interested reader to apply these conditions and the discussion as a whole, mutatis mutandis, to the other varieties of freedom fighting mentioned above. Since a revolution is usually understood as a successful rebellion, what I shall say here applies to rebellions, whether successful or unsuccessful.[2]

The *Shorter Oxford English Dictionary* defines revolution as "a complete overthrow of the established government in any country or state by those who were previously subject to it; a forcible substitution of a new ruler or form of government."[3] In this definition Peter Culvert discerns no less than four aspects of revolution:[4] (1) A certain *process*, which *may culminate in the revolutionary event. . . . or in a change of government by more peaceful means.*" (2) "A change in government (transition) at a clearly defined point in time by the use of armed force, or the credible threat of its use; namely, an *event*." (3) "A programme of change in either the political or the social institution of a state, or both . . . *after* a revolutionary event, the transition of power, has occurred." (4) "A political *myth*" giving the new political leadership "short-term status as the legitimate government of the state."

The conditions of a "just" revolution directly concern Culvert's aspects (1) and (2)—especially (2)—and only indirectly aspect (3). As he notes, the *Oxford English Dictionary* definition is the definition of a revolutionary *event*.

As in my discussion of the morality of terrorism in Chapter 2, the set of severally necessary and jointly sufficient conditions of a just revolutionary process and event that I shall stipulate here are again largely adapted from the relevant conditions of just war theory. Indeed, the relevant principles of a just war, many of which were adapted to terrorism, constitute necessary and sufficient conditions for morally justified "freedom fighting," whenever the fighting takes the form of a country's or people's war of liberation against foreign occupation or aggression.

Justification of the Application of Just War Principles to "Freedom Fighting"

In Chapter 3 I offered a justification for appealing to certain principles of just war theory in evaluating the morality of terrorism in Chapter 2. Here I shall similarly offer a justification for appealing to the principles of just war theory in evaluating the morality of freedom fighting. Following that, the pertinent principles will be discussed, to show how their satisfaction constitutes necessary and sufficient conditions for the moral rightness of freedom fighting, in its various forms.

For our immediate purpose it is necessary to exclude (defensive) war from consideration, since the question is whether the principles of just war theory apply—with the necessary changes—to those uprisings, rebellions and revolutions, civil war, coups d'etat, and guerrilla warfare that aim at freedom or liberation from domestic or foreign oppression and so qualify as "freedom fighting."

Although the principles under consideration have been expressly devised in relation to war and paradigmatically apply to it, some or all of them are, mutatis mutandis, applicable to "freedom fighting, just as some of them are applicable to terrorism. In fact, except for "competent authority," these princples relate to fundamental issues concerning the morality of the collective use of force or violence of considerably greater generality than war itself. As a consequence, they apply to the various forms of freedom fighting more directly than the analogical way in which, as we saw, some of them apply to terrorism.

The principles of (1) just cause and (2) right intention apply directly to freedom fighting. Indeed, by definition, "freedom has (1) a just cause, if one believes, as I do, that freedom from oppression is a moral purpose or end. Further, whether or not freedom is intended as an end or as a stepping stone to the establishment, say, of a dictatorship or some other oppressive rule, the concept of (2) right (and of wrong) intention clearly applies to freedom fighting.

Similarly, (3) innocent immunity, (4) proportionality, (5) necessity, (6) chance of success, (7) last resort, and (8) just peace are directly and without change applicable to all forms of freedom fighting. And, depending on the manner in which the force or violence is used in a particular case, the freedom fighting either satisfies or fails to satisfy one or more of these conditions. Thus (3) innocent immunity, (4) proportionality, (5) necessity, and (6) chance of sucess apply directly to freedom fighting, since it is patently wrong to use force or violence against innocents, or to harm noninnocents disproportionately to the intended political or military goals; or to do so when these goals can be peacefully attained, making the use of force or violence neither necessary nor a last resort. Similarly with (7) the principle of just peace, since as in the case of war, the victor is morally obligated to bring a just peace to the vanquished and other parties harmed by the use of force or violence.

Finally, and equally importantly, the rationale for the preceding principles, in relation to the different forms of "freedom fighting," is essentially the same as in the case of war.

Liberationist Revolution as a
Paradigm of "Freedom Fighting"

According to the *Oxford English Dictionary* definition, a revolution is the "complete overthrow of the established government . . . by those who were previously subject to it."[6] This unnecessarily restricts the meaning of "revolution," although the addition of "a forcible substitution of a new ruler or form of government" may be intended to allow for other possibilities. Although the definition covers revolutions instigated by citizens of a country C normally outside it, for example, by exiled dissidents, it does not cover possible revolutions brought about by noncitizens residing in C or even mere transients in the country and so "subject to it" only in a limited sense. It also fails to cover a revolution planned as part of a foreign invasion by another country, D, which has the support of C's citizens (e.g., if C's government is oppressive or is a foreign occupying power). The definition does however cover revolutions by the subjects that aim to overthrow a foreign occupying power.

In my view the conditions of a just revolution are the following:

1. If a revolution in a country C is conducted by citizens of C residing in it, or is instigated by citizens of C residing outside it, while C is fighting a war against another country D, any kind—especially any kind of military collaboration between the revolutionaries and D's government—can be morally justified only if D is fighting a just war: a fortiori, a defensive war. If *D* is an aggressor—in general, if it is fighting an unjust war against *C*—any collaboration with *D* by the revolutionaries would, at the very least, seriously damage any claim to a just revolutionary event. (Indeed, in the latter case the revolutionaries would not be *"freedom* fighters" at all.)

If the revolutionaries strike while *C* is engaged in an *unjust* war against another country, D, condition (1) above would not apply to it. The morality of the revolutionary event would then wholly depend on its satisfaction of the conditions below. These conditions would also apply, mutatis mutandis, if the revolutionary event takes place when *C* is at peace. They are:

2. *Just Cause*

The revolutionary freedom fighters would have a just cause if and when they and their compatriots, or a sizable part of the citizenry, *are* in fact oppressed or otherwise denied freedom by an indigenous or foreign power.[7] In general, the aim must be to create a political system that, as R. M. Hare puts it, is "better than the existing state," for example, provides greater equality of distribution.[8] Locke describes the "Just Cause" specifically as follows:[9]

> If a monarch seeks to rule without the legislative body, if he interferes with its work and liberty, if he changes the methods of electing the legislative without the consent of the people, if he delivers the people into the subjection of a foreign power, or, lastly, if he so neglects his executive duties as to cause the country to fall into a state of anarchy, then the people have a right to dismiss him.

3. Right Intention

In addition to having a just cause the revolutionaries must have a right intention; that is, their fighting must be *solely or at least primarily* motivated by or intended to achieve the freedom that is denied to them.

A government's or a political system's oppression of the citizens or subjects, its rampant inegalitarianism and injustice or other forms of evil, *prima facie* justify its overthrow by rebellion/revolution. Moreover, the redressing of these evils and the intention to do so are the only kind of state of affairs and the only kind of intention that can morally justify it. Even when a country's constitution guarantees its citizens the right to rebel, there is a serious question as to who would be morally or legally entitled to decide whether or not the majority or a sizable minority of the citizens or subjects, or certain prominent subjects or citizens, would be morally justified in rebelling. Clearly the targeted government or political system will almost certainly contest and resist, often by force, all attempts to overthrow it. As a result, only a very hazy and uncertain border area conceptually exists between justified rebellion/revolution, and (a) civil disobedience on the one hand and (b) lawlessness on the other hand. That is, the concept of rebellion/revolution is open in these "directions." But just as the purpose and intention of the individual who breaks an unjust law determines whether or not his or her action is civil disobedience (hence whether it is prima facie morally justifiable), so also the would-be revolutionaries' purpose and intention in overthrowing the government or political system—hence breaking the law—determines the *prima facie* rightness or wrongness of the rebellion/revolution. That is, determines it as far as the present condition is concerned.

4. Following O'Brien's formulation of proportionality as a political principle, the use of force by the rebels/revolutionaries, if unavoidable, must be *measured and restrained*. In fact it must be proportional, in the political sense, paralleling proportionality in *jus ad bellum*. *It must also* be proportional in Lackey's sense. As will be recalled from Chapter 2, the latter means that the probable, predictable evils of rebellion must be less—if possible considerably less—than the known existing evils the rebellion is intended to eliminate. In addition, the "military" principle of proportionality of *jus in bello* must also be satisfied. The overall cost in lives, property, resulting from the struggle must not exceed the military value or gains of the engagements in terms of the rebellion's ultimate goal, its just cause.

5. Sincere and resolute efforts should be made to avoid harming innocent persons. That is, the principle of civilian immunity in the stringent, "objective" form defended in Chapter 2 must be observed as consistently and thoroughly as humanly possible.

6. *Rebellion/revolution must be a last resort.* Conditions 4-6 are closely connected. A main reason for condition 6 is the great likelihood that lives will be lost and property destroyed from the almost certain resistance by the powers that be. Violence, the unlawful use of force, particularly the shedding of blood, is prima facie morally unjustified: it is *actually* wrong unless strong moral considerations in its favor outweigh the evils of violence. The injunction against *all* use of violence is defended by some either on religious or on secular grounds—in the latter case on, for example, absolutist deontological principles. But in addition to various well-known difficulties, ethical absolutism—if it consists in universal first-order and not universal second-order impartial rules[10]—is plagued by its inability to resolve possible conflicts between the moral rules it defends.

Universal pacifism maintains that all possible uses of force are wrong. But since pacifism cannot successfully be defended on consequentialist grounds,[11] including act- or rule-utilitarian grounds, the pacifist may appeal to human rights for support; for example, to the human right to life. The argument would go as follows: (a) human beings have a (an equal) human right to life, hence to their physical and emotional integrity; (b) an individual A's use of force against another individual B does not forfeit A's right to life; (c) B's special moral rights, some or all of which are inevitably violated by A's use of force against B, do *not* (indeed, cannot) override A's human right to life and to physical and emotional integrity.

Although I accept the premises of the argument,[12] they do not jointly entail the desired conclusion, namely, that it would be wrong for B to defend herself against A by using force. That conclusion follows from human-rights grounds only if it can be shown that the right to life—or any other human right for that matter—does *not* morally entitle one to defend or protect one's life, etc. by other than peaceful means: which is precisely one form of the very issue between pacifists and their critics. If the pacifist cannot show that the human right to life does not entitle one to defend or protect one's life by force, the case cannot successfully be made.[13] On rights theory the issue clearly hinges on the complex and difficult question of the extent and limits of a human right in general and of a given human right in particular. Consequently, the scope of its proper exercise in different circumstances.

With regard to rebellion/revolution the most desirable state of affairs in all respects would be a bloodless revolutionary event that also satisfies the other conditions of a just rebellion/revolution. But as I have said above, if force cannot be avoided to ensure success, it must be, among other things, measured and restrained in the ways specified. The actual, not just the intended damage inflicted on its target must be, as much as possible, close to the minimum necessary for success. Unnecessary force, and revenge or retaliation against the defeated heads of state and their followers, defenders, and supporters must be carefully avoided. The observance of these conditions should help enable the revolutionary event to satisfy the two proportionality conditions as well.

A fundamental reason why it is *prima facie* wrong to harm others is that it violates their human right to be treated as moral persons, including their positive (hence to a certain extent, negative) freedom and their right to be treated with consideration.[14] As already noted, some philosophers argue that a person's human right to life (if not also other human rights) is forfeited by his or her committing a serious crime. If true, that may justify the revolutionary's use of force against those in power and their supporters, since, ex hypothesi, they are noninnocent persons because of their unjust acts against the citizens or subjects. But for that to morally justify the revolutionary's use of force, the latter must be shown to be moral in principle. That, however, is precisely the basic issue!

A rule-utilitarian would provide an alternative justification of the use of force if it is assumed that in a particular case (a) the revolutionaries' cause is just, and if (b) revolutions generally have better overall consequences than the status quo. But we know that not all rebellions/revolutions that satisfy condition (a) satisfy condition (b).

Even when both conditions (a) and (b) are satisfied, not every kind or amount of force would be morally justifiable. As stated earlier, the force used must be "measured and restrained," and the resort to force by any morally and internationally interdicted weapons must be avoided. The former injunction can be understood as an application of the traditional just war theory's principle of proportionality in both its political and military senses, and the latter in enjoining a forceful response not exceeding the forceful resistance of the government's forces. In both forms of that principle, any force in excess of what is absolutely necessary cannot be justified in terms of the revolutionary just cause. It would be wanton violence, an exercise in sadism. It might also be wrong in terms of its probable postrevolutionary consequences, since the excessive use of force is likely to create such grudges and resentments in the vanquished survivors as to diminish or undermine the postrevolutionary regime's legitimacy. For instance, these survivors themselves may plot to avenge themselves by engineering a coup d'etat or counterrevolution. Excessive force may also undermine the citizens' or subjects' respect for the new government, rulers, or system.

7. Again, the revolutionaries must make resolute efforts to avoid harming innocent persons: civilians and members of the armed forces not directly involved in fighting the revolutionaries or otherwise actively opposing them; likewise farmers, factory workers, and others who supply the physical needs of the country and who are not directly involved in helping the government to resist the revolution. The deliberate harming, particularly the killing of these innocents as well as the unintended but knowing infliction of "collateral damage" on innocents is wrong and seriously jeopardizes the morality of the revolutionary event and the moral legitimacy of the new, revolutionary government.[15] The same goes for the threat to use nuclear weapons to deter a nuclear attack—if, as I firmly believe, the actual use of nuclear weapons is never morally justified.[16]

The principle of double effect cannot justify the harming, especially the killing of civilians, on the ground that, although knowingly performed, it is unintended; that is, whenever the agent's intention is to bring about overall good to the country as a whole, not to harm innocent persons—consequently, whenever he or she believes that the good aimed at outweighs the evil of harming innocent persons. For even in its most favored or plausible formulation, that principle fails, and in my view is morally unacceptable.[17]

The injunction that resolute efforts must be made to avoid harming innocent persons is an application of another traditional condition of just war theory: the principle of discrimination or noncombatant immunity. A justification of that principle may be sought in Anscombe's definition of murder as "the deliberate killing of the innocent"[18] together with the fact that by definition, murder is wrong. But the moral rule that the deliberate killing of the innocent is murder is, so to say, the flip side of the principle of double effect. Whether the rule that deliberately to kill an innocent person is to commit murder can be defended independently of the principle of double effect I do not know. In any case, Anscombe's blanket, absolutist definition of murder will not do. One serious problem with the definition is uncertainty about its scope. If we suppose that it it is exceptionless, then, given the further premise that murder is wrong, we get the imperative: "Do not deliberately kill innocent persons!" But Anscombe's definition may not (indeed, I believe that it does not) apply to absolutely *all* (kinds of) acts of deliberate killing of innocent persons. For instance, it can be cogently argued on consequentialist (including rule-utilitarian) as well as human rights grounds that it is morally justified to abort a fetus during the first and perhaps even the second trimester of pregnancy,[19] to save the pregnant woman's life or mental or physical health. It can also be argued, mutatis mutandis, on similar grounds that in certain extreme conditions voluntary active euthanasia,[20] suicide, and assisted suicide are morally right. In the case of suicide, I have in mind the sorts of extreme situations sketched by David Hume in his famous "Of Suicide."[21] Stated in general terms, although the rule that the deliberate killing of innocents is murder generally applies, it is not exceptionless—as in the kinds of cases mentioned above.

The principles of justice provide a straightforward justification of the principle of discrimination. In this case justice in the distribution of evils to the instruments and guardians of the putative oppressive status quo to be overthrown. For justice (and so, distributive justice in the broad, inclusive sense in which I am using the term) consists, as Plato and Aristotle said, in giving each person his or her due; consequently, in the case of distributive justice, what he or she deserves or is otherwise entitled to. Harming innocent persons is unjust since they do not deserve to being harmed. Indeed they are entitled to not being harmed.

8. A rebellion/revolution must be a last resort. It must be resorted to only after all reasonable peaceful means to the righting of the festering evils have been exhausted. In a *bona fide* democracy as opposed to a mere "facade democracy" or a "democracy" limited to an elite, moral grounds for rebellion rarely exist; since legal mechanisms designed to help redress such serious wrongs would be normally present. Rebellion/revolution is mainly defensible only in countries under foreign rule or suffering from dictatorial systems, where no (or no adequate) peaceful methods or mechanisms for the expression of popular dissatisfaction or protest exist. In the absence of such mechanisms they (ironically) lay the ground for sporadic acts and, ultimately, a last-resort general armed uprising or

rebellion.[22] The recent confrontation between Palestinians and Israelis in Israeli-occupied territories, triggered by Israel's opening of an exit for an ancient tunnel along the ancient Western Wall in East Jerusalem's Muslim Quarter, and the tensions between the Palestinians and the Jewish settlers in Hebron, are a clear signal of what may happen if violence erupts again and escalates.

9. If force is (must be) resorted to, the injury to the established government, etc. must be "real" and immediate."

10. *The rebellion must have a reasonable chance of success.* If the chances of success are slim, the rebellion should be called off, either permanently or until changing conditions make success much more likely. In the meantime the available nonviolent means, however meager, may be vigorously and systematically pursued to help achieve the desired change peacefully.

11. *The means the revolutionaries employ must be moral in their own right.* This condition limits the allowable means beyond those mentioned under condition 5, requiring that as much as possible the innocent should be spared. The present condition specifically prohibits the use of weapons or other lethal devices interdicted by multinational agreements or international law, including chemical and biological weapons, cluster and phosphorous bombs, and dum-dum bullets. (Above all, it prohibits the use of nuclear devices, which are the epitome of evil weapons, although unfortunately they have not been outlawed by international law.)[23] It also prohibits any appeal to terrorism as an instrument of rebellion/revolution, since—if the arguments in Chapters 2 and 4 are sound, terrorism is always wrong. Vandalism and looting or other forms of wanton destruction of property; rape, kidnapping, assassination and hostage-taking, whether part of terrorist activity or not, are also morally prohibited on this condition.[24]

One final point. A primary condition of a just war is that the war must be declared (or at least initiated) by the "duly constituted authority" in the country; for example, Congress in the case of the United States or Parliament in the case of England. But what would correspond to that condition in a rebellion? Clearly the "duly constituted authority" would be—or at least may conceivably be—the government to be overthrown, not the revolutionaries or their supporters. A Lockean as opposed to a Hobbesian social contract theory, which holds that sovereignty resides in the people, does resolve in principle this aspect of the problem of legitimacy for popular rebellions by giving the people—the majority—the moral and constitutional right to rebel whenever the government violates its trust to them. The question then is whether a further, twelfth condition of a just rebellion/revolution should be added stipulating that, to be morally justified, a rebellion/revolution must be supported, if indeed not initiated, by the majority of its citizens. An important practical consequence of adding such a condition is immediately clear: It would rule out many rebellions that, on the preceding eleven conditions, would be morally justified. The reason is simply that in the case of many successful rebellions a small group of activists initiate the revolutionary event, even when the rebellion gradually acquires wider, popular support. Moreover, history teaches that even when the majority comes round to supporting a rebellion, it rarely gets actively involved. The phrase "silent majority"— coined in a country that boasts of the people's right to near-absolute freedom of expression and very considerable freedom of action—reflects that fact. Again, change in attitudes and in political views comes slowly to the majority. (In a different context, the United States involvement in the Viet Nam War illustrates that fact. It will be recalled that more than a few years went by before the majority of Americans became unhappy with their country's military involvement and pressured their government to end the war.)

Although the democratic principle that political sovereignty resides in the people is eminently defensible, it is not clear that majority support is a *moral* condition of a just rebellion/ revolution. As far as the just cause and right intention conditions are concerned, the following stipulation would suffice: that (a) official abuses must be great enough to affect the country's majority; or if they affect only a minority, that (b) the hoped-for postrevolutionary order must be, at a minimum, designed for the benefit of the country as a whole. Indeed, in the case of (a), not just in the case of (b), a final condition (condition 12) of just rebellion is that, if successful, the rebellion (now revolution) must lead to a "just peace" for all concerned: that the rights of the revolution's survivors—the vanquished and their supporters as well as the victors and their supporters, or the people on whose behalf the revolution was actually or ostensibly fought—must be restored. This condition is an adaptation, in terms of rights, of the "just peace" condition stipulated by Douglas Lackey, earlier referred to.[25]

To sum up: After detailing the important differences between "freedom fighting" and terrorism, in order to show that the two are importantly different and should not be confused, the discussion concentrated on the moral assessment of freedom fighting. For that purpose it concentrated on rebellion/revolution, as a paradigm of freedom fighting, applying to it the just war principles and rules which provide necessary and sufficient conditions of "just," morally justified rebellion/revolution.

The model provided in relation to rebellion/revolution can be followed for the moral assessment of other forms of freedom fighting, such as liberationist uprisings, coups d'etat, civil wars, and guerrilla warfare. Because just war theory was historically formulated with an eye to war, a justification of the use of the principles/rules in regard to "freedom fighting" in general, was also included.

Notes

1. Burton M. Leiser, *Liberty, Justice, and Morals*, 2nd ed. (New York, 1979), 381. Italics in original.

2. The rest of this chapter is reproduced, with minor stylistic changes, from Haig Khatchadourian, "Just Revolution," in *Shaping Revolution*, Elspeth Attwooll, ed. (Aberdeen, 1991), 182-189.

3. It should be remembered that a rebellion/revolution may be completely bloodless. However, we are here concerned with the morality of nonpeaceful, violent rebellion/revolution.

4. Peter Culvert, *A Study in Revolution* (Oxford, 1970), 45. Italics in original.

5. Ibid., 5.

6. For an extended discussion of the concept of revolution, see David Beetham, *The Legitimation of Power* (Atlantic Highlands, NJ, 1991), especially ch. 7 (205-242)

7. Hannah Arendt, *On Revolution* (New York, 1965), 2, states that "the aim of revolution was, and always has been, freedom. Yet if it was amazing to see how the very word freedom could disappear from the revolutionary vocabulary, it has perhaps been no less astounding to watch how in recent years the idea of freedom has intruded itself into the center of the gravest of all present political debates, the discussion of war and of a justifiable use of violence."

8. R. M. Hare, "Justice and Equality," in *Justice: Alternative Political Perspectives*, James Sterba, ed. (Belmont, CA, 1981), 116. Liberty, or greater liberty for the citizens or subjects, may be another just revolutionary cause.

9. Quoted in R. I. Aaron, *John Locke* (Oxford, 1937), 285-286.

10. For, as Brian Barry shows in his *Justice as Impartiality* (Oxford, 1995), universal second-order impartiality does not entail universal first-order impartiality. See, for example, Barry's ch. 9, Levels of Impartiality.

11. See, for example, Richard Wasserstrom, "On the Morality of War: A Preliminary Inquiry," in *War and Morality*, R. Wasserstrom, ed. (Belmont, CA, 1970), 91ff. See also Haig Khatchadourian, "Pacifism," *World Futures*, 21, nos. 3/4 (1985): 263-278.

    I have said that universal pacifism cannot adequately be defended on utilitarian grounds. I think that is clear in the case of act-utilitarianism, since on that theory *some* uses of force in some actual or possible circumstances would serve the general welfare. Although perhaps less clear, universal pacifism also cannot adequately be defended on rule-utilitarian grounds, given the conditions that have prevailed in the world since humankind emerged from the jungle—or, at least, since the rise of the first civilizations. For, given these conditions, a rule that completely outlaws the use of force of any kind, in all actual and possible circumstances, would not generally—and certainly not always—serve the general welfare.

12.   Some moral philosophers (e.g. James Rachels and Douglas Lackey) hold that an individual who commits a serious wrong forfeits his or her right to life, but I have argued against that view. See Haig Khatchadourian, "Is Political Assassination Ever Morally Justified?" in *Assassination*, Harold Zellner, ed. (Cambridge, MA, 1975), 41-55. And see Haig Khatchadourian, "Terrorism and Morality," *Journal of Applied Philosophy*, 5, no. 2 (October 1988); reprinted in *Applied Philosophy: Morals and Metaphysics in Contemporary Debate*. Brenda Amond and Donald Hill, eds. (London, 1991), 113-128. See also chapters 2 and 6 of this book.

13.   See Khatchadourian, "Pacifism," for a partial discussion of the question whether the possession of a human right morally entitles the right-holder to use force or only peaceful means to protect or defend that right.

14.   See Haig Khatchadourian, "The Human Right to be Treated as a Person," *Journal of Value Inquiry*, 19 (1985), 183-195.

15.   Elizabeth Anscombe spells out well the distinction between the noninnocent and the innocent in her "War and Murder," in *War and Morality*, Richard Wasserstrom, ed. (Belmont, CA, 1970), 45. She writes: "What is required, for the people attacked to be non-innocent in the relevant sense, is that they should themselves be engaged in an objectively unjust proceeding which the attacker has the right to make his concern: or—the commonent case—should be unjustly attacking him. Then he can attack them with a view to stopping them; and also their supply lines and armament factories. But people whose mere existence and activity supporting existence by growing crops, making clothes, etc. constitute an impediment to him—such people are innocent and it is murderous to attack them or make them a target for attack which he judges will help him towards victory." See also Haig Khatchadourian, "Self-Defense and the Just War," *World Futures*, 20, nos. 3/4 (1985): 151-178, for an analysis of the concepts of innocence and noninnocence in relation to war.

16.   If the actual use of nuclear weapons is never morally justified, it follows that the threat to use them—even if only meant to deter nuclear or conventional aggression—is never morally justified. For the threat

to use nuclear weapons, except if it is a bluff, implies readiness and willingness actually to use them if attacked.

17. See Haig Khatchadourian, "Is the Principle of Double Effect Morally Acceptable?" *International Philosophical Quarterly*, 28, no. 1[109] (March 1988): 21-30, and Chapter 3 of this book. See also Fr. James F. Keenan's response to my criticism in his "Taking Aim at the Principle of Double Effect: A Reply to Khatchadourian," *International Philosophical Quarterly*, 28,no. 2[110] (June 1988): 201-205.

18. Anscombe, "War and Murder," 45.

19. In the case of rights, I have in mind the mother's human right to life, which outweighs the fetus' moral right to life when the fetus is still not a fully formed human being, anatomically and physiologically. Once it becomes a fully formed human being, i.e., in the third trimester, the fetus would have a human right to life equal to that of its mother's right.

20. See, for example, James Rachels' consequentialist defense of active euthanasia in his "Active and Passive Euthanasia," *Applied Ethics*, Peter Singer, ed. (Oxford, 1986), 29-35, and Chapter 3 of this book.

21. David Hume, "Of Suicide," reprinted in Peter Singer, *Applied Ethics*, 19-27.

22. The raison d'etre for rebellion would be limited to instances of the majority's blatant tyranny against a minority that is chronically discriminated against, as in the case of the black minority in the United States.

23. For arguments in support of the view that all uses of nuclear weapons in war are wrong, see, for example, Donald Wells, "The 'Just War' Justifies Too Much," in *Philosophy for a New Generation*, A. K. Bierman and James A. Gould, eds. (New York, 1970), 218-230, and Haig Khatchadourian, "Self-Defense and the Just War" (n. 16 above). Additionally, I maintain that threats to use nuclear weapons to deter aggression, not merely their actual use, are morally wrong.

24. See Chapter 3. For arguments against the moral justifiability of assassination, see Khatchadourian, "Is Political Assassination Ever Morally Justified?" (n. 12 above).

25. Ibid., 43-44.

Chapter 6

Responses to Terrorism

I

Broadly, two general kinds of responses to terrorism can be distinguished for our purposes: (1) "antiterrorist," and (2) "counterterrorist" measures and strategies, but using these terms—which are frequently used interchangeably—in a somewhat more restricted way than is common practice. Both antiterrorism and counterterrorism may be internal or external: employed by states domestically or transnationally, internationally. A state's internal and external antiterrorist measures and strategies are sometimes complementary, and so are its internal and external counterterrorist measures and strategies. The coordination of the two kinds of responses is essential for their success in deterring or preventing terrorism.

I shall employ "antiterrorism" to refer to the "administrative, police, . . . psychological resources, tactics, equipments, security, judicial and political measures"[1] employed by governments, together with the security measures taken by the private sector at airports, in airliners, at companies and corporations, etc., designed to prevent terrorist acts. In the case of governments, antiterrorist measures include the use of their judicial and penal systems as a whole to bring terrorists to justice. Thus antiterrorism has both a deterrent and a punitive aspect: to deter and so to prevent terrorism, to apprehend and bring to justice suspected terrorists, and to punish convicted terrorists.

As I use the word "antiterrorism," therefore, antiterrorist measures and strategies are, ideally speaking, nonviolent and in accord with the municipal legal systems of the particular states combating terrorism, and with extant international law concerning terrorism. Like measures and strategies designed by it to deter and to prevent crime and other forms of violence in general, a state's internal antiterrorist strategies and measures ideally consist of strategies and measures sanctioned by its municipal criminal law. Bilateral or multilateral extradition agreements with other states, and bilateral or multilateral conventions and agreements that outlaw various kinds of terrorist acts and activities, such as those created by the United Nations, provide additional mechanisms for combating terrorist activities. For example, agreements and conventions concerning hijacking, kidnapping and hostage-taking, air piracy, bombing, and killing.

In contrast to antiterrorism, "counterterrorism" in my restricted sense essentially involves the use of military force by an already existing state agency, such as the CIA in the United States, or by a secret governmental body specially designed to fight terrorism overtly and covertly. This aspect of "antiterrorist campaigns" by governments, draws on what Wilkinson describes as the state's "military and psychological resources, tactics, equipment. . . ."[2] Counterterrorism may include assassination of suspected terrorists, and air raids and bombings of hideouts and headquarters of suspected or known terrorist organizations by regular military units. To bring suspected terrorists to justice, it may also involve luring, abducting or kidnapping suspected terrrorists, rescuing hostages, and, in extreme cases, blockading, invading, and even declaring war on a terrorist state or a state sponsoring terrorist organizations.

The preceding characterization of counterterrorism is incomplete, since counterterrorist measures and strategies can also be used by terrorist states themselves against their own people as a whole or certain politically "undesirable" elements. What distinguishes counterterrorism from state terrorism and state-sponsored terrorism is that it is "monofocal" so to speak, not "bifocal." Targeting terrorists and their organizations is intended to help stamp out terrorism, not to intimidate or coerce terrorists, for example, by blackmailing them or extracting concessions from them. The distinction between immediate victims and victimized does not apply to it.

Ethical Issues of Antiterrorism and Counterterrorism

In considering the general principles of what he calls counterterrorist strategy, which includes both antiterrorism and counterterrorism in my usage, Wilkinson states that "the primary objective of counterterrorist strategy must be the protection and maintenance of liberal democracy and the rule of law. It cannot be sufficiently stressed that this aim overrides in importance even the objective of eliminating terrorism and political violence as such."[3] The ethical implications of this view are very important and will be considered in due course. As far as the liberal state is concerned, the truth of Wilkinson's foregoing view is I think beyond question. But what about undemocratic, especially totalitarian states? Clearly these states would be more than anxious to defend the status quo against all antigovernment movements—not least liberationist or revolutionary terrorism, for example, as part of a putative liberationist or democratic rebellion, coup d'etat, or civil war. If these goals are morally justifiable, as I believe they are, it would seem to follow that an undemocratic state would be morally in the wrong to seek to maintain the status quo. Yet if I am right in condemning all acts of terrorism, we seem to be driven to the seemingly paradoxical conclusion that even unjust states would be morally justified in combating terrorism or other unjust uses of force against it. That is, the evils of an oppressive state would not justify *morally wrong* attempts to destabilize or overthrow it by force,[4] although as Wilkinson points out: "neither terrorism [from below] nor any other mode of revolutionary struggle has much chance . . . in a totalitarian state."[5] (However, the overriding moral obligation such unjust states have would be to introduce democracy, peacefully relinquishing their absolute power. But that is a counsel of perfection rarely if ever followed in the real world.)

In general, even undemocratic, authoritarian states are morally justified in taking antiterrorist and counterterrorist measures, insofar as allowing the terrorism to go unchecked would harm innocent citizens, not insofar as it may destabilize their oppressive rule. But attempts to maintain the status quo by depriving the people of their rights would also be morally wrong. The sooner such states undertake the liberalization and democratization of their system, the better will be their chances of successfully combating uprisings and factional rebellions, or any domestic terrorism, by winning the majority of their peoples to their side and robbing the attempts to overthrow the status quo.

The opposite reasoning is characteristic of authoritarian governments. They typically argue that the violence must first be stamped out before the process of reform can begin; that that is their first duty and priority. They reason that to start the reforms while they are trying to end the violence would weaken them, making their success harder and perhaps impossible.[6]

I now turn to the moral evaluation of antiterrorist and counterterrorist measures and strategies in general, including those that governments and the private sector have practiced since the rise of modern terrorism several decades ago.

Ethical Issues Concerning Antiterrorism

Antiterrorism in general poses no special ethical problems, except in relation to the methods and procedures leading to the apprehension of suspected terrorists and their trial and possible conviction. There the ever-present danger lies in the suspension or abrogation of the normal legal defenses and protections of suspects and defendants in general, including suspected murderers. The most serious danger is that in their zeal to convict, the authorities may be tempted to torture suspected terrorists to extract confessions from them, or to assume that the suspected terrorists are guilty and to convict them before they are even brought to trial, in violation of the principle that a defendant is innocent until proven guilty.[7] Failure to read the suspects their rights and warn them against self-incrimination; search and seizure conducted without a warrant; interrogation in the absence of a defense counsel; and police intimidation or even brutality during interrogation, are chief among the legal rights that are in danger of being violated in these circumstances. Again, because terrorist killings, particularly of innocent persons, are widely perceived as cold-blooded murder, and because of the special repugnance judges and juries may feel toward terrorist acts, an added danger is the judges "throwing the book" at defendants convictd of terrorism, giving sentences more severe than those handed down to convicted murderers.

Wilkinson's following remarks, although directed to liberal democracies, eloquently summarize the dangers, such as the ones I have detailed, inherent in antiterrorist measures and strategies. He writes:[8]

> It must be a cardinal principle of liberal democracies in dealing with problems of civil violence and terrorism, however serious they may be, never to be tempted into using the methods of tyrants and totalitarians. Indiscriminate repression is totally incompatible with the liberal values of humanity, liberty and justice. It is a dangerous illusion to believe one can "protect" liberal democracy by suspending liberal rights and forms of government. Contemporary history abounds in examples of "emergency" or "military" rule carrying countries from democracy to dictatorship with irrevocable ease. What shall it profit a liberal democracy to be delivered from the stress of factional strife only to be cast under the iron heel of despotism?

Although the danger that democratic states may be destabilized by internal terrorism is miniscule compared to the danger of large-scale insurgencies such as rebellions or civil wars, Wilkinson's admonition regarding the suspension of a suspected terrorist's "liberal rights" should not be lightly dismissed. Governments must also guard against the paranoia of seeing a potential or actual terrorist in every foreigner, or even in citizens belonging to the particular ethnic, political, or religious group of known or suspected terrorists. Taking precautions (e.g., covert surveillance) to prevent terrorism is prudent and is morally justified as well as lawful in countries such as the United States, provided that they do not lead to the violation of innocent people's privacy and other legal and moral rights: above all, if they do not lead to scapegoating. The former danger is illustrated by a *Time* magazine report, 24 June 1991, 62, about Israel's use of "a work-permit card system, running on U.S. equipment, . . . to monitor the movement of Palestinians living in the occupied territories."[9] The article reported that "such systems are particularly attractive to governments troubled by civilian unrest. Guatemala, where death squads have been linked to hundreds of extrajudicial executions and "disappearances," purchased computer surveillance software from Israel in the early 1980's." *Time* further warned that "sale of these systems will continue to spread unless the U.S. and other vendor nations take steps to stop it. . . . At present . . . there are no regulations preventing the sale of relational-database systems to countries that lack basic constitutional safeguards." The article also quoted the complaint of Marc Rotenberg, the Washington director of Computer Professionals for Social Responsibility, that "The U.S. claims to have a role as the moral leader in protecting freedom and democracy. . . But we are becoming surveillance-technology merchants to the world." Here is a striking answer to the question of the moral responsibility of democratic countries raised earlier: in this case, of their responsibility not to be a party to the violation of the rights of people in countries fighting terrorism— including countries that practice terrorism themselves.

Ethical Issues Concerning Counterterrorism

Counterterrorism raises serious ethical issues; in the case of international terrorism, it raises serious legal issues as well. Counterterrorist bodies are secret arms of the security bodies or the military forces of countries combating terrorism and have the official blessing of their governments. This is true of the Israeli, United States, and various European counterterrorist units. Their activities are, in the main, deemed lawful relative to the particular legal system. In actual fact, at least some of the covert activities have no more claim to legality, strictly speaking, than do the CIA's cloak-and-dagger activities and its counterparts in other countries. Indeed, the covert activities of counterterrorist groups bear clear comparison with some of the past covert activities of the CIA, such as attempts on the life of various foreign diplomats or heads of state; the fomenting of uprisings, rebellions or coups d'etat against communist and other unfriendly regimes; and so on.[10]

In his discussion of responses to terrorism, Burton Leiser justifies counterterrorism on the ground that the vital interests of states targeted by terrorists are at stake. That fact, according to him, justifies unilateral or joint action by the targeted countries. But he greatly exaggerates the threat of terrorism and terrorist organizations "to every state's very existence," and goes as far as to call terrorists "enemies of mankind, a menace to world peace and order, and a threat to civilization." He adds, "The highest responsibility of any government lies in the protection of its citizens' lives", and describes the Israeli rescue at Entebbe Airport in Uganda as "a striking case of a government acting on that principle."[11] Consequently he urges[12] that

> The community of nations should explicitly recognize the right of any state to rescue its citizens in such situations, even though such rescue cannot be effected without an intrusion into the territory of a sovereign state. In the absence of such recognition, states whose citizens are in mortal peril as a result of such criminal behavior may resort to self-help to effect a rescue when other acceptable means of securing the hostages' release seem unlikely to be successful.

Leiser advocates various strong sanctions against states that sponsor or protect terrorists, ranging from "partial or complete interruption of economic relations, of . . . means of communication, and the severance of diplomatic relations to blockade, invasion or open warfare, . . . depending upon the gravity of the offence and the persistence of the offender in pursuing its policy."[13]

In "War and Murder," Elizabeth Anscombe defends society's coercive authority and power as essential to its existence: "For society is essential to human good; and society without coercive power is generally impossible."[14] Although her concern is with the morality of war, her defense of a society's use of force to preserve itself by just war can be readily extended, mutatis mutandis, to counterterrorism. That is, it might be argued that counterterrorist measures and strategies, as a form of (justifiable) national self-defence, would themselves be just whenever they are necessary for a state's/society's existence. This together with Leiser's claims, must now be examined.

Counterterrorism against Terrorist States and State-Sponsored Terrorism

Assuming for the sake of argument that *all* states, including rogue states, are morally entitled to protect themselves against all forceful attempts to destabilize them or threaten their existence (but see my earlier remarks in this chapter), Leiser's defense of the use of force by the target states against those states that harbor terrorists or sponsor terrorist attacks on them, would be morally justifiable on (1) act-utilitarian grounds, insofar as, under current conditions, *some* such forceful measures *may* have overall good consequences. They may either eliminate the terrorist groups and their camps or hideouts by such measures as air raids or commando operations, or militarily force the host states either to extradite the suspected terrorists or to try them themselves,[15] and end their sponsorship of terrorism. That is, assuming again for the sake of argument that national self-defence is always morally justified, the *means* Leiser advocates to further that end would also be justified. Whether these particular means would be likewise justified on (2) any adequate rule-utilitarian grounds, is harder to ascertain. As noted in Chapter 3, most (but not all) of the conditions considered in Chapters 2 and 4 can be adequately justified at least on general consequentialist grounds.[16] In any event, I believe that any adequate rule-utilitarian account of counterterrorism must stipulate and implement at least the following principles of just war theory.

First, the counterterrorists must have legally "competent authority," created and authorized—and carefully constrained or restrained—by the appropriate branch of government. Second, the operation must not deliberately target innocent persons, but must scrupulously avoid as much as humanly possible the knowing harming of innocent persons. Third, the purpose of the operations must be purely defensive. Fourth, they must be performed for the right reasons, with the right intentions, solely for the defensive purposes described. They must not be punitive or vengeful, motivated by a desire to incapacitate or destroy the offending state or its military structures. Therefore, fifth, the damage inflicted on the offender must be consistent, hence commensurate, with the just cause and the right intention. Finally, sixth, since the forceful measures are intended to eliminate the threat of terrorism at its source, the operation's overall purpose must be the establishment of a just peace, restoring the rights of all parties to the conflict.

The preceding effectively means that the conditions of a just war must also be satisfied, mutatis mutandis, by counterterrorist operations against terrorist and terrorist-sponsoring states. Such measures as invasion and war, or even air raids on terrorist holdouts or hideouts must be an absolutely last resort. They should be resorted to, if at all, only after all reasonable—preferably multilateral and international—diplomatic, economic, legal, and other pressures have been exhausted. A main function of the UN Security Council in the age of international terrorism should be, I believe, to use its diplomatic powers and prestige to try to prevail on offending states to cease and desist. The imposition of stringent economic sanctions, including blockades—the strongest forms of pressure that a nation or the UN can apply short of going to war—I find ethically most troublesome in the present type of case. It penalizes the country's vast majority, who are always innocent of terrorism. (See note 18 below.)

The situation is significantly different in the case of the UN embargo imposed on Iraq on August 2, 1990, to force it to withdraw from Kuwait, which is still in effect after the end of the Gulf War. It is different because the embargo was intended to avoid the UN coalition's having to go to war against the aggressor. Although it is the innocent masses that invariably suffer, and suffer most from such sanctions, as the subsequent situation in Iraq has shown, the cost of the alternative in terms of innocent and noninnocent suffering and lives would have been much greater. Indeed, that is what subsequently happened, particularly with regard to the Iraqi army and people, for Iraq refused to bow to the international pressure. And, less than six months after the embargo was imposed, the American administration claimed that it was not working or would not work and so launched the Gulf War before giving the sanctions a fair chance in the opinion of many Americans, including the present writer.[17]

Counterterrorism against Terrorist States

What I have said so far may give the impression that I endorse invasion and war as morally justifiable last resort measures in combating state and state-sponsored terrorism. In fact I have very strong moral objections to these highly destructive, extreme measures. I have already indicated my qualifications regarding various international sanctions, and my qualms about invasion and war are *a fortiori* still greater.[18] Such measures are disproportionate to terrorism's low-grade violence (as the United States government itself classifies terrorism). Terrorism has killed and maimed a comparatively small number of people, far fewer than the number of people killed in a single year in urban violence and crime in many American cities.[19] The greatest and widest impact of terrorism on the general population is not physical but psychological. At its heart is the continual fear it inspires. But despite their magnitude, the fear, anxiety, and uncertainty that haunt travelers, city dwellers, and others, and the other assorted evils of terrorist acts—perhaps most of all the harrowing experience of hostages and their families and friends—hardly ever justify in my view the unleashing of the hounds of war. As history teaches, the consequences of war are always extremely uncertain, and whatever good a war may result in almost never outweighs the destruction and death it wreaks on the innocent many, especially the young and elderly. That is, apart from the almost endless streams of refugees and displaced persons it creates. In short, the costs of war far outweigh the harms terrorism inflicts.[20]

These considerations also apply (although less forcefully in my view) to a targeted country's resorting to invasion or war to fight a *terrorist state* that practices terrorism against its own citizens or other countries. In both types of cases my reservations concerning blockades and economic embargoes are equally strong. In these cases blockades and embargoes would add to the misery and death toll of those very people for whose sake these radical measures are put in place, people who are already smarting from the official terrorism.

I believe that the morally most defensible response to non-nuclear terrorist states would be their isolation by the international community, preferably through measured UN sanctions involving the severing of commercial, diplomatic, and communication ties with them, freezing their overseas assets, sometimes in addition to restricting or completely banning imports from them. The nonviolent ways in which the United States responded to Iran's hostage taking of U.S. Embassy personnel in Teheran during the Carter administration, and the international sanctions imposed on South Africa's white apartheid regime, are good models for the future. Concerted action by the international community against a terrorist or terrorism-sponsoring state is always preferable to unilateral action by a nation targeted or otherwise harmed by international terrorism. It is, I believe, the *only* reasonable course in relation to a state that practices terrorism against its people. For then the problem becomes a global ethical-humanitarian one, not one limited to a particular country or state. The same applies to official terrorism by a state against ethnic minorities.

A government that continually uses state terrorism against a segment of its own population in the face of intense international pressure, would give the targeted population just cause for armed rebellion. If the other necessary conditions of a just rebellion or a just coup d'etat (as outlined in Chapter 5) are also satisfied at the time, the overthrow of the terrorist government would be morally justified.

Leiser is skeptical about the UN's ability to produce "concrete solutions to the international terrorist threat."[21] He blames what he calls the "obsession of the Arab and [former] Communist blocs with the Arab-Israeli dispute and [with what he thinks is] . . . their determination to expunge Israel from the community of nations" for what he alleges is the destruction of the UN's ability "to engage in creative endeavors to deal with terrorists and generally to improve the prospects for world peace."[22]

Leiser's words were written before the end of the cold war. Since then several significant events have demonstrtated that, if it has the support of the United States and its allies as well as Russia and China, the UN can become an effective international force in the cause of world peace. Its efforts to bring peace to war-torn countries such as Namibia and Thailand, and to help end the fighting among Serbia, Croatia, and the Muslims in Bosnia-Herzegovina, are important recent examples.

Let us return to terrorism. The release of the last American hostages held in Beirut through the UN's efforts demonstrates what patient, persistent, and skillful mediation can accomplish, although news stories also credited Iran with paying several million dollars to the hostage-holders in 1991 to release the remaining American hostages. A strong UN that enjoys the respect, support, and cooperation of the permanent members of the Security Council—above all the United States, Russia, and China—and, indeed, the entire world community of nations (assuming that to be possible) can be instrumental in bringing about a better world order than the "order" we have at present. The UN's resolutions regarding Iraq's invasion of Kuwait and the coalition's military action against Iraq can become a model of *last resort* concerted international response to all forms of tyranny and denial of human and other rights to oppressed peoples. The gradual transfer of central control of nuclear arsenals to the UN—at least of all strategic weapons possessed by the various members of the "nuclear club," not excluding the U.S. and the former U.S.S.R. republics that have nuclear weapons on their soil, would immeasurably diminish the danger of nuclear accidents and accidental war, as well as the danger of nuclear terrorism.[23] Unfortunately the chances of that happening in this century, if not at any future time, are I think nil.

Assassination and Terrorism

In "Is Political Assassination Ever Morally Right?"[24] I argued that on (a) rights grounds, and (b) act- and rule-utilitarian grounds, the assassination of political leaders for political reasons is never morally justified. With regard to (a), I argued that assassination violates the victim's human rights. True, some moral philosophers, for example, James Rachels and Douglas Lackey, maintain that individuals who commit heinous crimes forfeit their human right to life. If that were true, known (as opposed to merely suspected) terrorists would forfeit their right to life if they commit such acts as kidnapping, torturing, or killing their immediate victims. Consequently, their assassination for that very reason would not be wrong.

That argument will not do, however. It is meaningless to speak of a right one has simply as a human being, which is what a human right is by definition, as capable of being forfeited. Human rights cannot be "taken away" from any human being as long as he or she is alive, even if he or she happens to be in a deep coma, or is Hitler or Stalin. His or her human rights cease to exist only when death intervenes. It follows that if political assassination by private individuals or groups (leaving aside for later discussion the assassination of terrorists by agents of a state) is justifiable at all, it can only be so on some consequentialist, such as utilitarian, grounds.

Starting with act-utilitarianism, it is possible to conceive of circumstances in which some political assassinations would have overall good consequences for a particular country or even the world, such as Hitler's assassination during World War II. But political assassinations have in fact been almost always counterproductive, and I see no likelihood that situations will change so much in the world as to make political assassinations have the opposite outcomes. In the case of terrorists, resort to political assassinations tends to backfire even when the assassins escape punishment. Their cause tends to be damaged by the inevitable backlash from supporters of the fallen leader as well as those who hate violence in general. On the other hand, counterterrorist assassination of terrorists tends to unleash retaliatory terrorism, in the form of hostage-taking, bombings, skyjackings, and the like, since (like counterterrorists themselves) terrorists act on the "principle" of an eye for an eye and a tooth for a tooth—or worse.

The conclusion to be drawn from this is that, although political assassination can be theoretically justified on act-utilitarian grounds in very exceptional circumstances, a *rule-utiliarian* would need to adopt a rule against rather than in support of political assassination.

In addition to the preceding practical difficulties, political assassination is faced with serious theoretical problems in relation to both main forms of utilitarianism. One such problem is the great difficulty of ascertaining with any degree of precision the different sorts of circumstances in which political assassination would probably maximize the general welfare. To prevent its abuse the scope of its moral guidelines, whether conceived as mere practical (act-utilitarian) rules or as rule-utilitarian rules must be at least roughly delimited. To do so involves overcoming, at a minimum, two major difficulties. One, predicting the conditions under which these acts would tend to maximize the general welfare; and two, considering the inevitable restriction of their scope, the problem that the guidelines or rules arrived at would have little application in practice.

More specifically, a main consequentialist reason for outlawing political assassination is its potential for destabilizing a
country (something we witnessed for a while in India in the
wake of Rajiv Gandhi's assassination). An additional reason
for outlawing it is to discourage crackpots, publicity seekers,
fanatics, and madmen—those who have some real or imagined
grudge against particular political leaders, or who happen to
dislike them—from doing violence to them.

Again, who is to decide whether a particular political leader
deserves to be killed; or how evil such a person must be on
some particular consequentialist criterion or criteria, to deserve it? And who in the particular country would be the morally "right" person to commit that act? And what about "concerned" individuals elsewhere? Can they ever be morally
justified in assassinating, say, another country's putative evil
political head? For example, an American assassinating Fidel
Castro?

It might be thought that the relevant conditions of a just
war, duly modified or adapted, provide adequate rule-utilitarian conditions of justifiable political assassination; while the
nonconsequentialist who believes that political assassination
is sometimes right, can look on them as a body of applicable
deontological rules. A little reflection shows that with regard
to the political assassination by individuals or private groups
in a given country—such as the assassination of American presidents during the past two centuries, of Mahatma Gandhi, Martin Luther King, and Indira and Rajiv Gandhi—the above difficulties cannot be overcome by appeal to the conditions of a
just war, however ingeniously modified or adapted for present
purposes.

The foregoing discussion helps illuminate the question with
which we are directly concerned, namely, whether the (covert)
assassination of known or suspected terrorists by agents of a
state that appeals to self-defense or self-protection for justification, is ever morally justified. It is there that the appeal to
the relevant conditions of a just war would seem to offer greater
promise.

Since a country's right to self-defence or to self-protection
provides the moral basis on which counterterrorist measures
and strategies, including the ones I have enumerated, must, if

possible, be justified, I shall turn to a consideration of that right.

Self-defense, Self-protection, and Counterterrorism

The crux of the argument for counterterrorism is that it is a form of self-defense or self-protection: something to which every nation is morally and legally entitled. Two basic questions must be answered here: (1) whether counterterrorist measures and strategies are ever forms or instances of a country's self-defense or self-protection, and (2) whether national self-defense or self-protection is sometimes or always morally justified. These questions arise because the fact that terrorism is always wrong does not entail that a nation's appeal to just *any* possible means, particularly the use of force to combat terrorism, is always or even sometimes right.

To deal adequately with these questions the following related concepts must be distinguished: (i) a people, *nation*, or country, in the sense of "a relatively large group of people who share common customs, origins, history, and frequently language; nationality"[26] ; (ii) a nation's, people's or country's *political system*, such as democracy or dictatorship; and (iii) a *state*, in the sense of a nation's government at a particular time in its history.

I shall begin with the concepts of self-defense and self-protection. Governments, especially their military forces, are notorious for abusing the idea of (national) self-*defense* by deliberately stretching it beyond all reason whenever they take or are about to take military action against another country, or attempt to justify such action to their people and to the world. It is therefore best to avoid using the term in relation to counterterrorist measures and strategies.[27] Clarity would be gained if such acts as kidnapping, abducting or assassinating suspected terrorists, bombing suspected terrorist hideouts or villages in which they are believed to be ensconced, or blowing up houses suspected of sheltering terrorists, are thought of as ways in which a nation/state believes it is simply *protecting* itself against terrorism in general or the particular suspected terrorists and their suspected organizations. But as with

individual and group self-protection, the concept of nation/
state self-protection includes self-defense proper.

In answering question (1), whether counterterrorist measures
are ever self-defense/protection, I shall limit myself to considering whether the counterterrrorist measures and strategies I
have enumerated, all of which have been used by governments
fighting terrorism in recent years or decades, are morally right.

My answer is an unqualified No—as I have intimated by using the adjective "suspected" to qualify the word "terrorist"
and "terrorist organization." Just as everyone suspected of any
other crime is innocent until proven guilty in a duly constituted court of law, in a public trial, so suspected terrorists are
(or rather, ought to be considered) legally innocent unless and
until proven guilty. Morally speaking, this precludes attempts
to put an end to their activities or organizations by the aforementioned or by other violent methods. That leaves the ab-
duction or kidnapping of suspected terrorists at large as (possibly) the one morally defensible way of bringing suspected
terrorists to justice. In the case of suspected terrorists apprehended in a country other than the target country, extradition
treaties may succeed in bringing them to justice in the latter
country.

What about states that support or sponsor terrorism against
other states or their citizens? Here too my answer is that kidnapping, abducting or assassinating heads of state or other
high-ranking officials of suspected terrorist states would be
morally wrong. As for the morality of a target country's waging war in self-protection against a proven terrorist state, see
my earlier remarks about it in this chapter.

My negative answer is especially important in view of the
looseness and frequent misuse of the word "terrorist" that I
pointed out in earlier chapters; specifically, the current tendency of many governments, the media, and the general public to brand as "terrorist" any individual or group that opposes
them by violent means, often including in that class persons
or groups whose use of violence is morally justified. One practical reason for such all too common blanket condemnation of
any kind of forceful opposition to the established order as "terrorist activity" is rather obvious. It is simply easier to use such
ready-made labels than to try to examine each case on its own

merits; to discriminate between bona fide terrorists and others. But that is precisely one main reason why apprehended suspects must be given *proper* public trials.

Turning to question (2), whether national self-defense/protection is ever morally justified, my answer is briefly this: First, certain uses of force to deter domestic or international terrorism *are* morally right, provided they are essential for (a) the country's survival or its people's well-being; and/or (b) the protection of its political system if it is genuinely democratic and so, worthy of protection; and/or (c) the protection of the country's government if, once again, it is democratic, not oppressive, dictatorial.

A second main reason for my answer is that not all possible methods or strategies designed to protect a country's established political, economic and/or social order are necessarily moral: that order, or the country's rulers, may not be worthy of being protected. This is true apart from the fact that, not infrequently, corrupt rulers or governments appeal to "national security" in a blatant effort to deceive their people and perpetuate their own power. Or such an appeal to "national security" may be an excuse for a dominant minority's oppression of the majority. The same may be true when a dominant majority (mis)uses that notion to oppress the country's minorities.

A further reason for my answer rests on the fact that morally justifiable resistance to or attacks against a corrupt or oppressive government by nonterrorist fighters may be confused with (suspected) terrorists. In such circumstances appeals to national self-protection cannot be morally used as a blanket justification for the eradication of suspected terrorists. In its zeal to get rid of suspected terrorists, a nation may be tempted to trample on innocent people or destroy their hard-earned property. The same goes for the government's killing of innocent men, women and children by bombing their villages, or the blowing up of houses suspected of sheltering terrorists.

If the foregoing reasons are sound, the counterterrorist measures and strategies I have criticized are morally wrong, apart from whether the nation "protecting itself" by resorting to them is or is not itself moral. Consequently I shall next turn to what I believe are the necessary and sufficient conditions a nation-state must satisfy to be morally justified in protecting itself against violent threats to its survival, stability or integrity.

Once again it seems clear to me, that only the self-protection of a state or regime that possesses a modicum of moral and other positive values, particularly a state in which desirable moral qualities outweigh its moral flaws, is a moral good. If a state is, say, undemocratic, its attempts to preserve the status quo may be anything but a good. Here we must be careful to remember the distinction I mentioned earlier, between a country's people, and its economic, political, military, and legal systems, as well as its government at the time. Let us grant, as Anscombe says, that "*society* is [always] essential to human good, and society without coercive power is generally impossible." From that it does not follow that simply *any* state, however corrupt or evil, would be morally justified to "put down internal dissension, . . . [and] equally oppose external enemies"[29]. If the opposite were the case, the only necessary condition for (say) a just war would be that a state should be defending, or more generally, protecting itself against attack, which is untrue.[30] If it were true, no rebellion whatever against even the most corrupt state could ever be justified.[31]

The utilitarian (but not Anscombe, who is of course not a utilitarian) may retort that even when a nation's political system is unjust or its leaders are bad, the leaders' attempt to preserve the system and themselves may be the lesser of two evils. The outcome may be less bad in the long run than the destruction of property, bloodshed, instability, confusion, and lawlessness which normally attend attempts to overthrow the status quo. That would be true in relation to terrorism in particular, since its immediate targets more likely than not would be innocent private citizens who have nothing to do with the system or the government.

Against the backdrop of the foregoing discussion, and utilizing the earlier conditions (a), (b) and (c), my position can be summed up as follows. The existence of social organization, of human *society*, is decidedly a good, as Anscombe says. Human beings are social and political animals as Plato and Aristotle proclaimed, and society is instrumental in enabling human beings to realize their potentials and to satisfy their basic survival and social needs and interests. Even a bad society is a lesser evil than no society at all—than the breakdown of all social and political organization, such as Lebanon endured during its recent fifteen years of civil strife. All surviving societies are in some measure successful experiments at group living, at satisfying at least a modicum of human needs and realizing a modicum of human and individual potentialities. Consequently the preservation of any social organization, however flawed, is I believe preferable to a Hobbesian State of Nature, where anything like normal human life and relationships are well-nigh impossible. On consequentialist grounds, therefore, protectng the values that a society's existence makes possible against terrorism is morally right. The same is no less true on rights grounds. The members of any society have a human right to life. Anything that threatens that right—indeed, any other human right, such as the individual's right to freedom to strive to satisfy his or her basic human-*cum*-individual needs and interests and to realize his or her talents and other potentialities—is consequently wrong. As emphasized in Chapter 2, terrorism is a clear threat to these rights.

To sum up: This chapter has evaluated various measures and strategies initiated by governments in many parts of the world in response to the widespread incidence of terrorism during the past several decates. These measures and strategies designed to fight terrorism are of two general kinds: mainly judicial, "antiterrorist" measures and practices, and military, "counterterrorist" measures and strategies, designed to minimize or prevent terrorism and to punish terrorists. Both antiterrorism and counterterrorism, as they have been and continue to be employed by governments and state agencies, raise important, indeed disquieting, moral issues that were discussed in the chapter.

Starting with antiterrorism, the chapter considered various actual and potential abuses of the criminal justice system which can or do result from overzealous attempts to combat terrorism, including serious violations of the legal and human rights of suspects and defendants accused of terrorism. Among the abuses are the coercion and torture of suspects, or of their being convicted in the media and the forum of public opinion—sometimes in the minds of judges and juries—before they are brought to trial, even sometimes when they are at large or their identity is not known or is only guessed at.

The chapter next detailed the actual and potential abuse of the use of military force to combat terrorism: abuses that generally raise even more serious moral issues than antiterrorist measures.

Notes

1. Paul Wilkinson, *Terrorism and the Liberal State* (London, 1986), xiv. Wilkinson does not distinguish between "antiterrorism" and "counterterrorism," and includes the word "military" in a list of what he calls "antiterrorist-terrorist campaigns."

2. Ibid.

3. Ibid., 125.

4. Although political-moralistic/religious terrorism in these cases would have both just cause and right intention, it would violate the other conditions of morally justifiable uses of force.

5. Wilkinson, *Terrorism and the Liberal State*, 126.

6. It would be interesting to see how this argument has been actually used, e.g., by the present Netanyahu and the earlier Rabin administrations in Israel, in relation to the intifada and other forms of Palestinian resistance. (However, the intifada was not terrorist activity, and even the killings of Israeli soldiers by suspected members of Hamas may or may not be bona fide terrorist activities.)

7. The deportation in recent memory of Palestinians to the no-man's land between Israel and Lebanon without trial is a glaring example of this, leaving aside its violation of international law and the Geneva Convention. There are many recurrent examples of Palestinian activists held in Israeli jails for long periods without being charged and without trial.

8. Wilkinson, *Terrorism and the Liberal State*, 126.

9. "Technology: Peddling Big Brother," *Time*, 24 June 1991, 62.

10. See for instance Francis M. Wilhoit, "The Morality of National Intelligence: A Rejoinder," in *Values in Conflict*, Burton M. Leiser, ed. (New York, 1981), 423-429. Wilhoit's article is a convincing reply to Ray S. Cline's defense of the activities of the United States Central Intelligence Agency, "National Intelligence: A Moral Imperative," in the same work, 415-422.

11. Ibid., 395.

12. Ibid.

13. Ibid., 306.

14. Elizabeth Anscombe, "War and Murder," in *War and Morality*, Richard A. Wasserstrom, ed. (Belmont, CA, 1970), 43.

15.   Which is what present international law requires. But note the cointinuing impasse between the United States and Britain on one side and Libya on the other. The former demand that two Libyan intelligence officers implicated in the Lockerbie disaster be extradited to either the U.S.A. or Britain to stand trial. Libya has so far refused either to extradite them or to try them in its own country. Whether the UN embargo on Libya will finally force Colonel Kaddafi to extradite the two men remains to be seen.

16.   Some of these conditions follow from the concept or nature of "self-defense" itself. See Haig Khatchadourian, "Self-Defense and the Just War," *World Futures*, 20, nos. 3/4 (1985): 151-106.

17.   See Charles Webel, "Infantile Disorders Within the New World Order?" *New Ideas in Psychology*, 14, no. 1 (1996): 101-106. It is true that even with the embargo still in place, and after Iraq's disastrous defeat, Saddam Hussein has continued to resist the terms of the Un-imposed cease fire. But that does not constitute a valid argument against what I have said above, since rationality requires no more than acting in light of the evidence available to the agent at the time of deliberation and action.

18.   In fact my view is that no modern wars have been, or indeed could be, just wars, and that throughout history just wars could probably be counted on the fingers of one hand—and were probably fought with bows and arrows or stones.

19.   For instance, Leonard B. Weinberg and Paul B. Davis, *Introduction to Political Terrorism* (New York, 1989), 119-120, give the number of international terrorist attacks on United States citizens or property, 1968-1980, as 2863; the number of international terrorist incidents, 1968-1985 as 9552; and deaths caused by domestic terrorism in selected nations, as 9301.

20.   The two possible exceptions I can think of are nuclear terrorism from below or from above, if terrorists, or terrorist states are able to get hold of and threaten to detonate ncuelar bombs capable of killing millions of people. In that case, a war designed to prevent terrorists or terrorist states from implementing that threat, that also satisfies the other necessary conditions for a just war, would be morally justified.

21.   Burton M. Leiser, *Liberty, Justice, and Morals*, 2nd ed.(New York, 1979), 394.

22.   Ibid. Leiser does not explain how the "obsession" of the Arab states with the Arab-Israeli dispute has prevented the UN from engaging in creative endeavors to improve the prospects of world peace. It need only be noted here that no dispute of any kind—and the Arab-Israeli dispute is no exception—is a one-sided affair.

23. It should be added that the nuclear weapons placed under special UN control should never be used as a deterrent against aggression by any nation against another. For if the use of nuclear weapons is always morally wrong, as I have maintained in "Self-Defense and the Just War," the willingness to use nuclear weapons to deter aggression is also morally wrong. The same is true of threats to use nuclear weapons in order to deter aggression by nuclear or conventional weapons. On the other hand, threats intended as a bluff can be quite dangerous if a would-be aggressor nation calls the bluff, in addition to raising serious moral issues for the nations issuing the threat. The dangers I refer to include the possibility that if the bluff is called, the nations issuing the threat will be willy-nilly dragged into a nuclear or conventional war in order to save face, to preserve their prestige and "honor."

24. Haig Khatchadourian, "Is Political Assassination Ever Morally Right?" in *Assassination*, Harold Zellner, ed. (Boston, 1975), 41-55.

25. Note for instance the Bush administration's repeated expression of its hope for Saddam Hussein's assassination by "someone" in the Iraqi military, clearly implying that it makes no moral difference who does it so long as it is done. The idea is that Saddam Hussein is so evil that his assassination would result in a greater balance of good over evil: presumably for Iraq, the region, and Western interests.

26. "Nation," *American Heritage Dictionary*, 2nd College ed.

27. For an analysis of the concepts of individual, group, and national self-defense, see Haig Khatchadourian, "Self-Defense and the Just War."

28. Anscombe, "War and Murder," 43. Italics added.

29. Ibid. One problem with Anscombe's discussion is that she uses "society," "the rulers," and "a country" interchangeably, which leads to the non sequiturs she commits.

30. The fact that Anscombe distinguishes between "attack" and "aggression," and so does not equate a nation's being attacked with its being morally in the right shows that, in *that* connection, she does distinguish morally justified and unjustifed self-defense (in general, self-protection) in relation to nations or countries.

31. A related question is whether an evil state is morally entitled to punish those who break its laws. Part of the answer depends on whether the laws themselves are just.

Chapter 7

Conclusion

Contemporary terrorism is one of the many scourges of the
twentieth century, a century distinguished by a pervasive
maladie d'esprit and violence unprecedented in magnitude and
inhumanity in the annals of history. Although terrorism is a
relatively low-level form of violence and its victims and victimized have mercifully been far fewer than the victims of the
many wars, civil wars, rebellions, revolutions and—most of all—
the genocides in this century, its psychological effects on the
general public far exceeds its destruction of life and property.
General anxiety and fear have become almost synonymous with
the word, particularly for travelers, office workers, shoppers,
and other innocents, in many parts of the world. In any discussion of the subject, a clear understanding of what terrorism is
and is not is therefore essential, particularly as the misconceptions about what it is are presently so widespread in the media, among politicians and other public officials, for the person in the street, and even for many scholars. The word
"terrorism"—the mere mention of which now tends to evoke
anxiety and vague fears in people's minds—has at the same
time become fashionable with politicians, the media, and the
general public, so that all sorts of violent acts and activities by
individuals and groups, as well as by certain countries, are almost automatically labeled "terrorism," often when there is
little or no evidence to support the labeling, or even when the
violence is something other than terrorism.

As a highly (almost always, negatively) charged emotive word,
"terrorism" serves as a convenient verbal weapon of governments, rulers, and private organizations and institutions that

are the targets of force or violence of almost any kind: in the case of governments, political rulers, or regimes by those who seek to sabotage, destabilize, discredit, or even overthrow them. By indiscriminately calling almost any use of force or violence against them "terrorism," including genuine instances of "freedom fighting," the targeted governments, rulers, or regimes are able to justify its suppression by whatever legal or extra-legal means they have, ignoring its real nature and causes, especially whatever underlying economic, social, political, religious, or other root causes it may have.

On the other hand, bona fide terrorists, in trying to justify their violence and to win adherents to their cause, often capitalize on the more positive emotive coloring of "freedom fighting" and declare that they are not terrorists but "freedom fighters."

Since a proper understanding of the nature of terrorism is the essential first step in properly evaluating its morality and in properly responding to it, Chapter 1 was devoted to that task. Besides attempting to show what terrorism is not, it attempted to show, through a careful analysis of the concept of terrorism, what terrorism is. It was seen that terrorism consists of a number of major types and forms, defined by the nature of their goals and distinguished from other types or forms of violence by a common "bifocal" nature. The bifocal character of terrorism consists in the fact that the acts of violence against their "immediate victims" are but a means for the perpetrators' attainment of their real goal, which is to pressure or coerce their real targets or the "victimized"—that is, particular individuals, groups, countries, governments, etc.— to accede to their political, moralistic, religious, or other kinds of demands.

Other important features of the concept of terrorism in general, such as its vagueness and "openness," were also discussed in Chapter 1.

Surprisingly few scholars and, especially, professional moral philosophers have concerned themselves with the moral evaluation of terrorism; and some of the evaluations that have been made have been vitiated by misconceptions of the nature of terrorism. To remedy that deficiency, chapters 2 and 4, together with the appendix to Chapter 4, were devoted to the task, in terms of the applicable principles and rules of contemporary "just war" theory, fundamental human rights (as developed by the author in other writings), and consequentialist—specifically, act- and rule-utilitarian—principles.

One common and important misconception of terrorism results from a lack of clarity about the difference between terrorism and "freedom fighting"—liberationist uprisings, rebellions and revolutions, civil wars and guerrilla warfare. The confusion between terrorism and "freedom fighting" has sometimes led to the defense of terrorism as morally justifiable, at least in some cases. Chapter 5 was therefore devoted to distinguishing "freedom fighting" from terrorism, providing a positive analytical concept of the former, and laying out the necessary and sufficient conditions for morally justifiable "freedom fighting" in terms of the applicable just war principles and rules.

Because the application of just war theory to terrorism and to "freedom fighting" is a relatively novel approach in the book, a justification for it was provided in chapters 3 and 5. A consequentialist justification of the principles of just war theory, except the absolute principle of innocent immunity, was also provided in Chapter 3.

An adequate account of terrorism (as well as of "freedom fighting") requires an understanding of the forces—especially the historical-cultural root causes—that give rise to it. For that purpose a fairly long appendix is provided (pages 141-170), outlining the history of the Palestine Problem as a case study of root causes of political-moralistic/religious terrorism in the particular case of the Palestinian-Israeli conflict, and of the Arab-Israeli conflict as a whole.

Finally, Chapter 6 addressed the question of the morality of various judicial, antiterrorist, and military, counterterrorist measures and strategies employed by various countries to combat terrorism. It also cautioned the sometimes overzealous judicial systems and counterterrorist agencies about the danger of violating people's, including suspected terrorists', moral or legal rights, in their effort to apprehend, prosecute, and punish perpetrators and masterminds of terrorist acts, and/or to penalize states that commit or sponsor terrorism.

Thus although terrorism is a menace, and always morally wrong as well as unlawful—hence should be appropriately responded to—Chapter 6 stressed that responses to it must be legally justifiable and scrupulously moral. In particular, that the powers that be should never forget that anyone suspected or tried for any crime, however heinous, is presumed innocent unless and until the evidence, presented in a just and fair public trial, shows otherwise. Moreover, that in pursuing the elusive goal of stamping out terrorism, the authorities must guard against practicing the abhorrent "guilt by association," in relation to the compatriots or coreligionists of suspected or convicted terrorists.

Appendix

The Palestine Problem:
A Case Study of Root Causes of
Political-Moralistic/Religious Terrorism

I

In Chapter 1 I briefly mentioned the historical and cultural, including socioeconomic root causes of political and moralistic terrorism, as constituting one of the at least five important aspects or elements that an adequate description of terrorism must include. Indeed, an understanding of the rise or existence of these types of terrorism is impossible without a proper understanding of their root causes, just as effective responses to these types of terrorism are always difficult and sometimes impossible without the elimination of their root causes. To understand the forces that lead certain groups to forge terrorist organizations and to commit political, moralistic, or religious terrorism given certain precipitating factors, it is essential to know the nature of those longstanding circumstances, such as (perceived) injustices or grievances, that drive individuals or groups to place themselves and others in harm's way by performing acts of terroristic violence.

"Root causes"—a concept that applies to the types of terrorism I noted—need to be distinguished from the "precipitants" of all types and forms of terrorism without exception.[1] The precipitants are the "combinations of factors . . . at work in these years [from the late 1960s on] which transformed terrorism from a relatively minor annoyance into the global attention-getting phenomenon it is today." They are "specific events that precede and indeed stimulate the use of terrorism." On the other hand, what I call root causes or what Weinberg and Davis (vaguely) call "preconditions," are those circumstances or states of affairs "that set the stage for terrorism."

Knowledge of whether particular acts of *violence* have root causes or only precipitants is essential, first, for knowing whether or not they are "bifocal" and so whether they are acts of *terrorism* or of other types of violence to begin with.[2] Second, knowledge of the *type* of terrorism involved in particular cases of terrorism—whether it is predatory, retaliatory, or political and/or moralistic/religious terrorism and hence the appropriate response to it—requires an understanding of the perpetrators' reasons, motives, or goals for their terrorist acts.

Frequently, the longstanding grievances or injustices which constitute the root causes of political, moralistic, or other terrorism are territorial, or territorial-religious in nature. "Mau Mau" terrorism in Kenya from 1952 to 1956, directed "principally against the [British] colonial government and the European settlers",[3] the ongoing IRA terrorism in Northern Ireland and in England, and Basque terrorism in Spain, are familiar contemporary examples of *domestic* political, or political/moralistic, or moralistic/religious terrorism, while the Palestine Problem—the near-century-old territorial dispute between Arabs and Jews regarding what used to be Palestine— is the root cause of international Palestinian and other Arab political-moralistic terrorism, as well as a root cause of Iranian and Libyan state-sponsored terrorism.

Not all terrorism from below or from above is territorial or territorial-religious. The (unsuccessful) violence of the Russian terrorists in late nineteenth century Russia, which was intended to demoralize the autocratic Tsarist regime, is a good example of the former. The Libyan-sponsored terrorism against European and American interests (which may have included the downing of the TWA plane over Lockerbie) was, I think, mainly in retaliation against European and American support for Israel, and only indirectly territorial at best, in the sense that it may have also been intended as a show of support for the Arab cause in general and the Palestinian cause in particular vis a vis Israel. Similarly, Iran-sponsored international terrorism—as opposed to Iran's support for Hezbollah guerrillas in Southern Lebanon, which is, on the whole, an example of "freedom fighting," not terrorism—has not been territorial but retaliatory: a sponsorship of attacks on international United States (and Israeli?) interests.

Because of its complexity, its international character, and its global implications and world-wide consequences, I have chosen to outline the Palestine Problem in this appendix as a case study of root causes of political and related terrorism, to dramatize and concretely illustrate the importance of an understanding of the root causes of such terrorism in general. Traversing that tragic period in the history of the Middle East and beyond is also instructive in helping the reader to appreciate the bitterness, resentment, and anger, the frustrations and desperation which, given certain precipitating conditions, may drive members of a community or people to acts of terrorism or other forms of violence against what they perceive to be the cause or causes of their sorry state. In the case of Palestinian terrorism, that is essential for undersanding how a pacific people who docilely endured for centuries the Dark Age of Ottoman rule and, with only sporadic outbreaks of violence, the subsequent British Mandate over Palestine, could give rise to terrorism—and more recently to the intifada, after the defeat of the Arabs for the second time, in the 1967 Six Day War.

There exists a great deal of misunderstanding as well as disinformation and propaganda on all sides of the Arab-Israeli conflict, including distortion and misuse of historical and other pertinent facts[4] as well as (as we saw earlier in this book) of such key concepts as *terrorism, counterterrorism, and freedom fighting*, together with their deployment as political weapons.

As with the most searing classical tragedies, the territorial conflict between Palestinian and Jew is not between right and wrong but between right and right; between the historical moral/legal rights of the Palestinians and the moral/legal rights of the Jews: a fact now widely recognized in the West and among moderate Palestinians and Israelis. This renders the conflict especially poignant, without, however, in any degree or manner morally excusing or justifying terrorist acts stemming from the conflict, inasmuch as (as I have argued in this book) nothing ever morally justifies terrorist acts. But their moral/legal claims have led some Palestinians—at least the more radical among them—to the conviction that what Israelis and the West condemn as terrorism is actually justifiable "freedom fighting."

II

In "Criteria of Territorial Rights of Peoples and Nations"[5] I distinguished several fundamental moral/legal criteria of territorial rights (T-criteria) of nations and peoples, of which three are relevant here. The first of these is the "first or original settler criterion" (OSC), which I described as the "primary criterion of territoriality, and so the historical basis of all other valid or bona fide T-criteria."[6] Further:

> We can in fact say that "original settlement of a land" defines the concept of a T-right to a territory. Logically, however, it can be regarded as just one historically very important sub-form of a more general criterion; viz. that a people 'P' or a nation 'N' that has continuously occupied a territory 'T' before another people 'O' or nation 'M,' has a moral and a de jure legal right to 'T': a right that 'O' or 'M' either entirely lack or (whenever the latter has some right to it) has a weaker degree or form than it. We can call this criterion the "Earlier Settler Criterion" or ESC.

A second criterion is what I called the "nonoriginal or secondary settler criterion" (SSC). The third relevant criterion consists in a people's acquiring a moral right to a territory it occupies "if it is given to it by a nation-[state], e.g. a colonial power that was ruling it [,] or by an international body such as the UN, which has the moral and legal authority to do so."[7]

The basic moral claim to a Jewish state in Palestine essentially rests on the fact that part of the country was the biblical land of Israel, the one and only homeland of the Jewish people, although the people of Israel were not the country's original settlers. In other words, the claim rests on the Jews' satisfaction of the "secondary settler criterion," SSC. The fact that except for a small minority the Jews did not reside continuously in the territory for almost two thousand years, does not diminish their territorial rights on SSC. The crucial reason is that Jews did not leave the country of their own accord but were expelled by order of the Emperor Tiberius, and is in my view at the heart of their rightful claim to a Jewish state in part of Palestine. Had the majority left of their own free will, the Jewish claim (leaving aside the religious claim that God promised Judaea and Samaria to the people of Israel[8]) would have lost much if not all of its moral validity. The fact that an Arab majority continuously resided in the territory since A.D. 634, when Palestine was conquered by the forces of the Omayyad Khalid ibn Walid, would have given the latter a decisive moral claim to the entire territory and against any Jewish moral claims to any part of it as a putative national home or potential Jewish state.

The Palestinians' moral entitlement to a share in (indeed, perhaps to half of) the land rests on the following facts. First, as stated earlier, they have lived continuously in that land since the Arab consquest in the seventh century. Second, they constituted the majority of its inhabitants at the time of Israel's creation in 1948. To that extent the Palestinians also satisfy SSC. I say "to that extent" since SSC would have been fully satisfied had the indigenous people at the time of the Muslim conquest vacated it of its own accord or had simply ceased to exist.

That, of course, did not occur. The Arabs under Caliph Abu Bakr conquered the country and its then-indigenous people. Since the Jews too acquired what became the land of Israel by force of arms against the indigenous Philistines and Caananites, they too fail fully to satisfy OSC, but satisfy (or fail to satisfy it) in the same degree as the Arabs.

The equal or roughly equal degree in which the disputants satisfy SSC enables us to avoid (a) the thorny general question of whether conquest of another's land is ever morally justified, and whether (b) the Jews' conquest of parts of Caanan and the Arab conquest of Palestine were morally justified. But if the answer to (a) is Yes, SSC would have to be modified to allow for morally justifiable conquests.

Whatever the answer to these questions, there is an important third point directly relevant to the Palestinians' and the Jews' territorial claims—this time to their legal territorial claims. I refer to the 1947 UN Partition Resolution, which gave equal legal rights to Jews and Palestinians, and satisfies our third criterion of moral/legal territorial claims.

III

The following outline of the Palestine Problem will attempt to sketch selected Palestinian and other Arab perceptions, feelings, and attitudes about what they have consistently viewed, from about the dawn of this century—particularly from the Balfour Declaration of 1917—as the grievous injustices suffered by the Palestinian people. These injustices include, prominently, the UN Partition Plan and the creation of the state of Israel in 1948, and the latter's occupation of the West Bank, the Gaza Strip, and East Jerusalem from 1967 when it conquered them, until recently, when Israel granted autonomy to the Palestinians in Gaza and the West Bank, including eighty percent of Hebron, under PLO leadership, with the exception of East Jerusalem.

Britain and the Palestine Problem

The origins of the Palestinian people are still a matter of historical uncertainty, although there exist various hypotheses concerning the matter.[9] But it is a historical fact that the Palestinians, the great majority of whom have been Arabs, go back at least to the Arab conquest of the country in A.D. 634. Thus they have been its indigenous inhabitants and the great majority of descendants continued to live in the land, long before the influx of European Jews from the Diaspora during World War II. Yet even with that influx during the British Mandate, the Jews continued to be a small though growing minority of the country's population, as the accompanying table shows. I have already noted the significance of these facts for the territorial claims of Arabs and Jews.

Population Increase in Palestine, 1922-1945[10]

	Jewish Population	Non-Jewish Population	Total Population
1922	83,790	668,258	752,048
1945	554,329	1,255,708	1,810,037
% Growth 1922-1945	569%	87%	140%

Calculated on the basis of Gertz, pp. 46-97.

On November 2, 1917 the Balfour Declaration burst like a bomb upon the Palestinian population. In that fateful declaration A.J. Lord Balfour, then British Foreign Secretary, in a letter to Lord Rothschild, stated that "he had been authorized by the British government to release a statement indicating that 'His Majesty's Government view with favour the establishment in Palestine of a national home for the Jewish people, and will use their best endeavours to facilitate the achievement of this object, it being clearly understood that nothing shall be done which may prejudice the civil and religious rights of existing non-Jewish communities in Palestine, or the rights and political status enjoyed by Jews in any other country.'"[11]

Discussions at cabinet level and consultation with Jewish leaders, including Dr. Chaim Weizmann, whom Philip Groisser describes as "a leading British scientist and Zionist," helped negotiate the declaration.[12]

Britain's action of promising a "national home" to the Jews in a land that was not part of its own territory, disregarding the desire of the country's Arab majority for nationhood, was seen by the latter as highhanded and completely arbitrary, at a time when England had not even been granted a League of Nations mandate over the country!

But if the British government lacked the legal and moral authority in 1917 to promise the Jews a national home in Palestine, did it acquire such an authority after the end of World War I, when the League of Nations granted Britain a mandate over Palestine?

The Palestinians' attitude toward the Balfour Declaration and, by implication, their answer to this question, is well stated by Edward Said:[13]

> The Declaration was made (a) by a European power, (b) about a non-European territory, (c) in a flat disregard of both the presence and the wishes of the native majority resident in that territory, and (d) it took the form of a promise about the same territory to another foreign group,[14] so that this foreign group might, quite literally, *make* the territory a national home for the Jewish people.

And:

> Balfour's statements in the declaration take for granted the higher right of a colonial power to dispose of a territory as it saw fit. As

Balfour himself averred, this was especially true when dealing with such a significant territory as Palestine and with such a momentous idea as the Zionist idea, which saw itself as doing no less than reclaiming a territory promised originally by God to the Jewish people, at the same time as it foresaw an end to the Jewish problem.

It should be added that these criticisms of Britain's action entail nothing either positive or negative concerning the moral rights of the Jewish people to a national home. As I have maintained previously in this appendix, the Jews, like the Palestinians, have a significant moral claim to part of the land.

What magnified the Arabs' sense of injustice, their consternation and suspicions aroused by the Balfour Declaration and its implications, was that the Declaration came almost simultaneously with the Bolsheviks' leakage of the secret Sykes-Picot agreement between Britain and France when they came to power in Russia in 1917, in a deliberate attempt to embarrass the allies of the Tsarist regime. As Anthony Nutting states, the Arabs saw the situation as nothing short of betrayal, since during World War I they strongly believed that the British had promised them certain parts of the Near East (including Palestine) in return for their help to defeat the Ottomans.[16]

The twists and turns of British foreign policy in its attempts to win Hussein ibn Ali, the Grand Sherif of Mecca, to the British side both before and after October 31, 1914, the day Turkey declared war against Britian and entered the war on Germany's side, are well-summarized by Anthony Nutting in Chapter 24, "The Arab Revolt," in *The Arabs*.[17] Nutting writes that in October 1914,

On the outbreak of war between Britain and Germany, [Lord] Kitchener, now Secretary of State for War in the British Cabinet, sent Abdullah [one of Hussein's sons] a message to inquire whether, if Turkey joined Germany against Britain, the Grand Sherif would cast his lot with the Turks or with the British . . . . Britain was at war with a deadly enemy and needed the Arabs as her allies. This was the chance for which Hussein was waiting.

As a result of further correspondence between Hussein and Britain in October 1915, Sir Henry McMahon, speaking for the British government, wrote to Hussein that "Britain would recognize the areas in the Sherif's previous note [i.e., "the proclamation of an Arab caliphate for Islam"] with the exception of certain areas . . . listed as (1) the Cilician districts of Mersin and Alexandretta, (2) Lebanon and part of Syria west of a line between Aleppo and Damascus, and (3) Southern Iraq from Baghdad to Basra"[18]

Despite his repeated attempts, and despite Faisal's successful revolt against Turkey, Hussein failed to pin down Britain to a precise definition of frontiers. Nutting summarizes the final position as follows:[19]

> The upshot of all this was very far from the precise definitions of the Damascus memorandum. Though nothing can excuse Britain's and France's subsequent deception of the Arabs by the secret Sykes-Picot agreement and the Balfour Declaration, it seems extraordinary that the Sherif should have regarded these exchanges as an adequate guarantee on which to launch the Arab Revolt . . . . Hussein clearly wanted to believe in Britain's sense of fair play because he wanted the revolt, which depended entirely on supplies of British arms and ammunitions for its success.

Adam M. Garfinkle summarizes the situation thus:[20]

> When war erupted in 1914, Britain and Ottoman Turkey found themselves on opposite sides. The British attempted to use any means, fair or foul, to turn the non-Turkish inhabitants of the empire, many of whom had been at the edge of rebellion even before the war began, against their increasingly harsh and capricious masters in Istambul. In the course of this effort, the British made many promises, some of them mutually exclusive, to the Arabs and to the Jews. In return for aiding the British war effort against the Turks, London promised the Arabs political independence. The promise to the Jews, brokered by Dr. Weizmann, who as a chemist had aided the British war effort, was the Balfour Declaration of November 1917.

More important for an understanding of the causes of the Arabs' issue with Britain in the early part of the century than the vague and ambiguous British promises to them[21] were the British views and perceptions of the promises, and the Arabs' consequent anger when they discovered what they saw as Britain's double dealing in relation to them and the Jews.

Again, in mandating to Britain and France to rule over the Near East provinces of the former Ottoman Empire, the League of Nations intended for these countries to give eventual independence to their peoples. In failing to grant independence to the Palestinians, Britain went against that very mandate.[22]

What Anthony Nutting calls "a footnote to the [twentieth century] history of Palestine" is *a propos* at this point, with regard to "the road not taken" by history. He writes:[23]

> One curious reflection prompts itself. Had France and not Britain succeeded in grabbing Palestine after World War I, Palestine might well have become an independent Arab state in the same way as Syria and Lebanon . . . . Rather than a "national home" for the Jews, Palestine would have become a French protectorate. And, when the time came for the Arabs to rise and throw off the French yoke, the Palestine Arabs would have made common cause with their Lebanese and Syrian brothers in gaining their independence. With the state of Palestine preserved intact, the whole Middle East would then have gained in stability and in strength.

In short, the extreme vagueness of the words "national home" (which paralleled the vagueness of the earlier British promise, or "promise," to the Arabs) augured nothing but future trouble and conflict, and became a major contributor to what the Zionists perceived the promise to entail.

The Arabs lost no time in voicing their strong opposition to the Balfour declaration, Jewish immigration into the country, and the building of increasing numbers of so-called Jewish colonies, in the decades preceding Israel's independence. Despite Arab protests, demonstrations, and other forms of resistance to British policy, including some guerrilla fighting against British forces in the 1930s, some Arab farmers continued to sell their land to the Jews, attracted by the high prices they were being offered, until their leaders belatedly forbade such sales.

For their own political ends, Palestinian leaders and the leaders of the neighboring Arab states played a not insignificant role in what became, in the words of a distinguished Lebanese historian, a veritable "catastrophe." They did so first and foremost by their outright rejection of the partition plan. This, together with the creation of the state of Israel, led to the first of a series of Arab wars against the new state, and played a crucial role in the ensuing half-century of bloody conflict, suffering, and loss for all concerned, and continues (albeit in a lesser degree) to this very day.

During the Mandate the endemic political disagreements and conflicts between the Palestinian nationalists and leaders

of that time, and their intransigence and unwillingness to com-
promise, scuttled all British attempts to lead Palestine toward
independence under the League of Nations rules. Thus in 1922
they rejected the British proposal to hold general elections
for a legislative council proportionately represented by Christians, Muslims, and Jews (and the same happened with later
British plans), because they thought that it would legitimize,
as Garfinkle put it: "A Zionist political share in the governing
of Palestine. They also forced Arab members to withdraw from
other British-devised advisory councils, foiling all early attempts by the British to create a basis for communal power
sharing."[24] They insisted, among other things, on the forma-
tion of a government based on simple majority rule, which
would favor the Arabs, as well as the "abolition of the principle of Jewish national home, [and] an end to Jewish immigration" That particular uncompromising position continued
until 1948. Garfinkle adds that "the only real difference of
importance was that while, in the 1920s, the Arabs imagined
that they might expel the Zionist settlements from Palestine
entirely, by the late 1930s and 1940s they strove to minimize
the growing size and strength of the Yishuv and prevent Jewish political autonomy."

As we have seen, the Palestinian leaders and the leaders of
the neighboring Arab states had the prime responsibility for
the Palestinian and general Arab stand toward British policy
in Palestine, since it was they who decided the fate of ordinary
Palestinians throughout the Mandate. Ordinary Palestinians
had no opportunity—for example, by means of referendums
or plebiscites—to decide for themselves the crucial issues affecting their and their children's very existence and future.
Worse still, in the same arbitrary and highhanded way their
leaders and heads of the neighboring Arab States, decided in
1948 for the Palestinian people by invading the nascent state
of Israel rather than accepting partition.

The personal and political rivalries between the Palestinian
leadership that, from 1920 on, helped prevent the creation of
an independent Palestinian state in 1948, were specifically
between two prominent and powerful Jerusalem Muslim families, the al-Husseini and the Nashashibi families. In 1937 the
rivalries led to the final Palestinian rejection of the British

Peel Commission report. That report proposed that "the Gali-
lee, with the exception of Nazareth, and the north coastal plain
would be a Jewish state. The Arab state would include everything else, save for a wide corridor from Jerusalem to Jaffa,
which, with the Nazareth enclave and bases on the sea of Gali-
lee and at Aqaba, would remain in British hands. The Arab
state was to be joined, though it was not specified exactly how,
with Abdallah's realm in Transjordan."[25]

The proposal was rejected outright by al-Husseini and the
Arabs of Syria and Iraq, "because it granted . . . Jewish sovereignty in any part of Palestine. Publicly, Abdallah and the
Nashashibis opposed it as well, but privately it was known that
they favored the plan so long as Raghib an-Nashashibi would
rule under Abdallah at the expense of the al-Husseinis."[26]

The Zionists were also divided on the Peel Commission report. Similar Arab attitudes continued to be manifested in the
post-Peel commission period. For instance, when after 1937
the British agreed in principle to the main Arab demand for
an independent state under majority rule, the Arabs refused
to acknowledge any Jewish rights "to special protection and
rights for the Jewish minority. In the end there was no agreement and the British dictated their own terms."[27] One casualty
was the dropping of the idea of an independent Arab state,
which was dropped "at least for the time being. A White Paper
containing these strictures [including British accession to Arab
demands to end Jewish immigration and to curtail land sale to
Jews] was issued in May 1939. . . . Both the Jews and the Arab
Higher Committee rejected the White Paper."[28] To top it all,
Palestinian nationalists led by Haj Amin al-Husseini sided with
Nazi Germany and the Axis powers during the Second World
War. In addition to its immorality, that meant the loss of a
valuable opportunity for the Arabs to fight on the Allies' side—
which had a just cause and, at least, one main right intention,
however morally flawed Allied fighting against the Axis powers came to be in terms of the rules of *jus in bello*. By contrast,
the Jews seized the opportunity. A Jewish brigade was formed
and fought alongside the Allies, thereby gaining valuable experience with war that later served them well.

The same pattern of rejections I have described—sometimes
unilateral, sometimes bilateral—and the continued deadlock

over the country's future, were repeated in relation to Britain's final effort to solve the Palestine Problem: the Morrison-Grady Plan and "subsequent patchwork attempts to adjust it in various ways"[29] failed. Finally, in May 1947 Britain turned over the whole matter to the United Nations—with the results we all know. The Zionists but not the Arabs accepted the principle of partition plan "with passion."[30]

The unrelenting bombast and rhetoric of the leaders of the Arab countries neighboring Israel about their vaunted military prowess and supposed ability to defeat the Jewish state with ease, in 1948, 1967, 1972,[31] and (in the case of Iraq) in 1991, repeatedly created false hopes in the Palestinian masses that were dashed to the ground. This helped make the Arabs their own worst enemies. By siding with Saddam Hussein against Kuwait during the 1991 Persian Gulf War—although that was a psychologically understandable expression of anger and frustration at their miserable condition—the Palestinians residing in the occupied territories demonstrated once again their tendency to be swayed by external Arab blandishments, despite their belated awakening to the fact that they had to forge their own future themselves, that they must rely on themselves first and foremost.[32] I refer of course to, among other things, the grassroots movement[33] of Palestinian civil disobedience and the intifada that erupted in 1989 in the occupied territories, and their determination, reflected in the more recent PLO partnership with Rabin and Peres in the peace process, to forge their own future and destiny.

One must not of course forget Palestinian terrorism, as an even earlier form of grassroots resistance to the occupation than the intifada. But I believe that it was not Palestinian terrorism but the 1982 Israeli invasion of Lebanon, coupled with Israel's later attempts to crush the intifada, that resulted in greater sympathy for, or empathy with, the Palestinians' plight and their cause.

A heavy price has been paid by the Palestinian people because of its and its leaders' longtime gullibility and naiveté, and political inexperience in believing the assurances and declarations of the Arab States. (Essentially the proverbial psychology of a drowning person clutching at straws, greatly magnified.) To that must be added the debilitating phenomenon of "make-believe" which, with some notable exceptions, has been endemic to Middle Eastern society:[34] the pronounced tendency to live in a world of fantasy or make-believe, and the inability or perhaps unwillingness to face reality—resulting in a tendency to profound self-deception. Fortunately, things have changed in recent years, especially with Oslo I and II, in which the PLO and most Palestinians have shown much greater realism than before.

The United States and Israel

So far I have sketched the highlights of Arab actions, attitudes and reactions to British Palestine policy from 1917 on; in order to show the crucial role played by Britain in relation to the Palestine Problem. I shall now turn to the role of the United States in the creation of Israel and its unwavering policy towards that state since then, because that is the source of the deep Arab resentment of and hostility toward the U.S. government and foreign policy from 1947 on, making Americans and American interests worldwide a main target of Palestinian and other Arab (as well as, to some extent, Libyan and Iranian) terrorism.

The role of the United States in the creation of Israel and its unflagging support for it ever since is all too familiar and needs no elaboration. It is a commonplace that President Truman recognized the new state minutes after it proclaimed independence on May 15, 1948, and that the U.S. government's economic and military aid to Israel has been the largest given to any foreign country.[35]

Perhaps less known is the Truman administration's role in the passage of the UN Partition Resolution of November 29, 1947: the pressure it applied on a number of reluctant Latin American countries (who wanted to see Jerusalem internationalized) to vote in support of the Resolution. Even less generally known I think is the long-standing American sympathy for the "redemption of Zion" going back to the nineteenth century. Philip Groisser observes how the Bible's influence on Christian thinking led Christians and Jews to give their support for "'the redemption of Zion' even before the present-day Zionist movement was established in 1897."[36] Thus in 1818

President John Adams expressed his desire to see the "reestablishment of an independent state for 'the Jews in Judea.' In
1844 Mordecai Manuel Noah, an American Jew who had served
as United States consul in Tunis, asked the Christian world to
help Jews resettle in Palestine . . . . In 1891 a petition to President Benjamin Harrison presented by the Reverend William
Blackstone and signed by many leaders in public life, the
church, the press, and the business world called for an international conference to 'consider the Israelite claim to Palestine as part of their ancient home' and an 'inalienable possession from which they were expelled by force.'"[37] Presidents
William McKinley, Theodore Roosevelt, and William Taft also
expressed sympathy "for the idea of reestablishing Palestine
as a homeland for the Jews" shortly after the Zionist movement was organized.[38]

I have mentioned the crucial role of the United States in the
creation of the state of Israel and its economic and military
aid to Israel as major reasons for general Arab hostility toward and frustration with American Middle East policy—which,
until recently, has marred American-Arab relations and has
made American interests a target of international Arab as well
as Libyan (and Iranian) terrorism. Of particular concern to
Arabs has been the enormous military aid to Israel since its
creation, which helped make possible its stunning victories over
the Arabs in the 1967 and 1972 wars. Until recently, another
major source of Arab anger has been the United States' lack of
evenhandedness in its Middle East policy—a policy the Arabs
perceived as "made in Israel," with the "tail wagging the dog."[39]
Yet another source of Arab anger has been the steadfast refusal of successive American administrations, in agreement
with the hard-line Israeli position, to contemplate the idea of
an independent Palestinian State in the occupied territories.[40]
In fact, from the beginning, the Arab masses have seen Israel
as nothing but "the tool of American (neo-)colonialism" (*'amilat
al-isti'mar*), serving America's imperialist economic and strategic interests; a thorn thrust in the side of the Arabs. They
have seen what they regard as complete indifference on the
part of successive U.S. administrations to the heavy price the
Palestinians have been paying for half a century, in terms of
continual Israeli exploitation and humiliation, and material

and spiritual deprivation, and (except when American interests were or are affected) to the region's economic, social and political upheavals and instability.

In the 1970s the Palestinian leadership, focusing on the issue of the justice of the Palestinian territorial claims, as well as to some extent on the Jews' historical territorial claims, proposed the creation of a secular, democratic Palestinian-Jewish state. That it paid scant attention to the proposal's impracticality is evident from the pages of a collection of essays titled *Toward Peace in Palestine*. The collection included Yasser Arafat's speech to the UN, "The United Nations Appeal for Peace,"[41] as well as articles by a number of prominent Arab activists and intellectuals. The essays make it clear that their authors—which included such well-known Palestinian intellectuals as Fayez Sayegh and Edward Said—considered the proposal as providing a "most ethical and just" solution to the Palestinian problem. The writers believed it gave both Palestinians and Jews that to which they were morally and legally entitled. That is crystal clear, for example, in the following passages concerning what Hatem I. Hussaini called "a new society in Palestine."[42]

> Very few people can argue the morality or the legality of an Israeli state at the expense of the Palestinian people. This is why Israeli leaders avoid this complex issue by simply saying that the Palestinians do not exist.

And,

> The Palestinian leadership have proposed a partnership with the Jews, an equal sharing of the land. The concept of a secular, democratic State in Palestine where Jews, Christians and Muslims coexist with equal rights is a most ethical and just solution to the complex, prolonged conflict.

From a moral and legal point of view, what is particularly significant about the second passage is the idea of equal territorial rights for Palestinians and Jews, implicit in the proposal for the equal sharing of the land. Note too Hussaini's succeeding statement: "In a lasting peace, the Israeli people must have full and equal rights."[43] In making the one-state proposal the

Palestinian leadership clearly went a long way in recognizing the extent of Jewish territorial rights.

Hussaini is not unaware of the practical problems facing the proposal, and observes that some have deemed the concept "impractical and unrealistic."[44]But immediately after he digresses in a revealing non sequitur by adding: "yet very few can argue against the principle itself." More pertinent however is the justification that follows: "Moreover, this solution is much better than continued conflict, war and suffering. Other more realistic solutions, like dividing the country into two, are not based on real coexistence and true equality and thus would no doubt lead to future conflict and war." Toward the end of his essay Hussaini goes along with what he calls the PLO's acceptance of "the establishment of its authority on a part of Palestine, the West Bank and Gaza, in an attempt to give the Palestinians there some form of freedom and human dignity." But he continues to stress that "the concept of a secular, democratic humanist State where Jews, Christians and Muslims can coexist in peace and equality is the most durable and lasting solution."

A suggestion similar to the PLO's one-state proposal of the 1970s was made by a Jewish writer, Norton Mezvinsky:[45]

> The solution of the fundamental problem of the Arab-Israeli conflict is the de-Zionization of the State of Israel. This proposal, which points farther past peaceful destruction of the Zionist state to the establishment of a secular, democratic, multi-racial state, will not solve all the problems for all the people in the Middle East, but it could be one concrete and positive step forward for at least some few millions of people in this troubled area of the world.

The one-state proposal was swiftly rejected by Israel as amounting to the destruction of the State of Israel.[46]

The one-state proposal was subsequently replaced by a two-state proposal by Arafat and various Palestinian intellectuals, and became the official position of the PLO's 19th National Council or Parliament, in November 1988. In 1996, under strong pressure from Prime Minister Peres, the Palestinian National Council struck the article advocating the destruction of Israel from the Palestinian Charter. In that way the Pales-

tinian Authority finally gave de jure recognition to Israel's right
to exist.

The Role of Israel

Having briefly sketched Britian's and the United States' roles
in the creation and evolution of the Palestine Problem, I finally turn to Israel's actions and policies from 1967 until very
recently in relation to the occupied territories, and its contribution to Palestinian political and retaliatory terrorism and
other forms of violence, including the intifada.

Israel's role essentially began with its occupation of the West
Bank, the Gaza Strip, and East Jerusalem, and its iron-fisted
military rule of these territories until the partial Palestinian
autonomy. It included Israel's gradual de facto annexation of
East Jerusalem and relentless de facto annexation of parts of
the occupied territories by the building of Jewish settlements
there: a process of "creating facts on the ground" that continued even during Shimon Peres' tenure as foreign minister and
as prime minister, and is expected to continue even more ag-
gressively under the new Israeli government.

The following are a few other examples of Israeli actions
and policies vis-a-vis Palestinians in the occupied territories
that have enraged, and embittered, and increasingly alienated
the Palestinian population: the violation of the Palestinian
population's basic moral (e.g., human) and civil rights by the
periodic closings of Palestinian schools and colleges; the ex-
pulsion and deportation of over four hundred suspected members of Hamas (some of whom were later allowed to return);
the bone shattering beating and shooting of the "stone children" *during the intifada*; the blowing up or bulldozing of the
houses of suspected Palestinian terrorists; the torture of Palestinian prisoners and terorist suspects;[47] the imprisonment
without trial of Palestinian dissidents; the repeated bombing
of southern Lebanese villages suspected of harboring Shi'ite
Muslim, Party of God (Hezbollah) "terrorists"[48] or radical Palestinian guerrillas, causing the death or wounding of innocent villagers. To these should be added Israeli clandestine
counterterrorist measures outside Israel, which have resulted
in the assassination of leading PLO figures and of the spiritual leader of the Shi'ites in southern Lebanon.

These and other activities, viewed by Israel as acts of self-defense against terrorism, continued during the various stages of the Israel-Palestinian peace talks. For instance, in the introduction to a publication titled *The Price of Peace: The Toll of the Peace Process on Palestinians in the Occupied Territories, 1 Nov 1991–15 Feb 1992*,[49] which appeared after the Madrid peace talks, the authors mention Israel's continued "seizure of land, uprooting of trees, and construction of housing, commercial zones and roads for settlers."[50] The rest of the booklet details "Israeli Policies Against the Palestinian Civilian Population." It mentions the number of Palestinians killed or injured by the Israeli army and settlers since the beginning of the intifada; the arrests, raids and torture in detention; curfew and other movement restrictions; expulsions; interference with Palestinian education; taxation causing "extreme financial hardship for Palestinians; and demolitions and house sealings."[51] It goes on to describe Israeli land seizure and settlement of specific parts of the occupied territories, and "settler violence,"[52] since the start of the Madrid conference;[53] and, finally, "media disinformation."[54]

The foregoing facts—those that relate to the period before the start of the peace talks in November 1991, the period between November 1991 and February 1992, and the period after February 1992—dramatize some of the major reasons for Palestinian resistance to Israel since 1967, incuding terrorism. According to his campaign speeches and his post-election statements, the present Israeli Prime Minister, Benjamin Netanyahu, has said No to the return of the Golan Heights to Syria, and to an independent Palestinian state with East Jerusalem as its capital. With Palestinian autonomy, Israeli military incursions into the autonomous areas in hot pursuit of suspected terrorists has ended, perhaps temporarily, but Netanyahu does not rule them out if further terrorist attacks occur—like the series of bloody suicide bombings that occurred in rapid succession before his election.[55] It has been reported that Netanyahu is not "enthusiastic about initiating a 'hot pursuit' policy that would send Isareli troops after terrorist suspects even if the latter fled to Palestinian-controlled areas. Such moves could provoke confrontation with Palestinian police, perhaps outright guerrilla war."[56] It was also reported that Netanyahu "believes the country's best hope for increased security lies in continu-

ing cooperation between Israeli and PLO security forces. 'What
is clear from the experience of the last few months—since the
spate of bombings in Jerusalem and Tel Aviv—is that the Palestinian Authority has the ability to control terrorism and to
prevent these kinds of attacks against Israel. This is what we
expect them to do,' says Netanyahu. 'We reserve, of course,
the right to act in our own self-defense, at any time, as the
need arises. [But] this does not nullify their obligation to do
what they have been showing they can do—keeping a check on
violent surges by Hamas and the Islamic Jihad.'"⁵⁷

With security uppermost in Israeli minds and with a yearn-
ing for a place in the sun in Palestinian hearts, but with
Netanyahu "a reluctant supporter of the historic negotiatons
with the Palestine Liberation Organization",⁵⁸ the prospects
for a lasting peace in the area seem more uncertain than they
were, or seemed, just before May 29, 1996, the date of the
Israeli elections. The specter of a repetition of the past cycles
of Hamas and Islamic Jihad terrorism and swift, ruthless Israeli retaliation—followed by terrorist counterretaliation and
further Israeli retaliation—or even a second intifada, is beginning to loom again on the horizon. The possibility also exists
for worsening relations between Israel and the Arab nations,
including Egypt and Jordan with whom Israel has a peace treaty.
Indeed, Arab leaders meeting in Cairo soon after the Israeli
elections "warned . . . that they would 'reconsider the steps
taken toward Israel' in recent years if that country's new government did not totally withdraw from captured Arab lands."⁵⁹
As for relations with Syria, Netanyahu's No to the return of
the Golan Heights to Syria, if it does not change, will almost
certainly doom an agreement with Syria.⁶⁰

The final communique of the Cairo Arab summit demanded
that—"Israel's new prime minister, . . . adhere to the principle
of 'land for peace,' which they [the Arab countries] see as the
basis for a comprehensive settlement of the Arab-Israeli conflict [endorsed by the Clinton administration].

"Among other things, the leaders demanded a full Israeli
withdral from the West Bank and Golan Heights, the removal
of Jewish settlements from those terrritories; the establishment
of a Palestinian state with East Jerusalem as the capital; and
Israeli recognition of the 'right of return' for Palestinian refugees displaced in the Arab-Israeli wars."⁶¹

Despite his continued hard-line stance, the *Newsweek* inter-viewer saw in Netanyahu's comments "a more nuanced—and hopeful—approach. The peace process remains, but Netanyahu envisages a different process. He is willing to talk and to com-promise. He's willing even to leave open the question of trad-ing land for peace, but only if an eventual deal provides genu-ine peace of mind for his people. 'What is peace if not the achievement of tranquillity?' Netanyahu asks. 'If the accompa-niment of so-called peace involves continued flare-ups, bus bombings, violence and terrorism, this is not peace.'"[62]

Netanyahu also noted that it was the hard-line Likud leader Menachem Begin "who signed a treaty with Egypt two years" after his election in 1977. "'It turned out differently,' says the new prime minister. 'They are saying [similar things] about me today—and things will likely turn out differently.'"[63]

Despite the preceding statements of the newly elected Prime Minister, Yitzak Rabin's assassination in early 1996, tragically dramatized the deep split—a split down the middle—that ex-isted in Israel between those who wanted to continue the peace process and those who passionately opposed it, indeed, wanted to roll it back. The split was dramatized again in 1996 with the defeat of Shimon Peres' labor government and the election of Netanyahu's hard-line government. The split appears to con-tinue as I write, and is most visible with regard to the with-drawal of the Israeli army from the greater part of Hebron, to which it is committed by the Oslo-Cairo peace accords. De-spite the recent long-drawn, on-and-off negotiations between Netanyahu's government and the PLO representaives, medi-ated by the United States, no agreement has so far been reached. As recently as November 16, 1996, the *Milwaukee Jour-nal-Sentinel* carried an Associated Press report, "Jews Protest Plans to Pull Troops from Hebron," stating that "tnsions [are] high as Israeli settlers, Palestinians await [the] outcome of regotiations." It added: "In Jerusalem, dozens of settlers and members of the right-wing group Women in Green rallied outside Netanyahu's office on Friday [November 15] to pro-test the emerging Hebron accord. Jewish settlers said they felt betrayed." One of the protestors said the agreement "forecloses the future of the Jewish community in Hebron." The report noted that "the new Hebron deal—like the old one—gives the Palestinian-controlled municipality authority over issuing building permits, thus making it difficult for the Jewish enclaves to expand" as Netanyahu had promised during his election campaign.

As if the increased tensions that the new Israeli government's hard-line position ushered in were not enough, in late September 1996 the Israeli government secretly opened a new exit to an archeological tunnel along the ancient West Wall of East Jerusalem. It did so without informing Yasser Arafat or consulting King Hussein, the official guardian of the Muslim Holy sites in East Jerusalem. The bloodshed that ensued, in which Palestinian police fired on Israeli soldiers firing on Palestinian demonstrators outside the Al-Aqsa compound, raised tensions between Israel and the Palestinians to a higher pitch than at any time since the Hamas suicide bombings just before the new Israeli elections. According to the Associated Press, as reported in the October 20, 1996, issue of the *Milwaukee Journal-Sentinel* in a column titled "Disputed Tunnel a Tourist Hot Spot": "Muslim authorities, alarmed by extremist Jewish groups that seek to resurrect the Jewish temple on the Al-Aqsa compound, contend the tunnel is a physical danger. They say it has caused cracks in 700-year-old Islamic buildings. Muslims also say they were angered by the new exit because Israel did not consult them about making a significant change affecting the area around the Al-Aqsa complex. The mosque compound, which was built on the site of the Jewish temple is one of Islam's [the third] holiest sites."

The bloodshed—with fifteen Israelis and sixty Palestinians dead—led to widespread fears that the peace process was about to unravel, and led President Clinton to call a hastily arranged, largely unsuccessful Washington summit to try to salvage it. The fighting also led to a UN Security Council resolution which called on Israelis and Palestinians "to immediately halt hostilities and resume peace talks."[64]

Meanwhile, on the outskirts of Jerusalem, "Yizhak Rabin's grave has become a place of pilgrimage for Israelis who yearn for the peace that 'could have been'." They are anguished "over the bloody fighting between the two peoples that seems to have wiped out any hope for peace. . . . Some of the visitors . . . blamed Netanyahu and his refusal to make concessions to the Palestinians for the violence that has killed dozens of people.

'Rabin has been remurdered in the past few days because all of his ideas are dying,' said a student. Another visitor said: 'This is a shrine of regret for what could have been. . . . He [Rabin] was the last chance we had.'"[65]

A week before the Al-Aqsa "exit" incident, "a conference of Arab States repeated an earlier charge [stated earlier, p. 160] that Israel was breaking the peace agreement by a) closing of borders [between Israel on the one hand and the West Bank and Gaza strip on the other]; b) failing to withdraw from towns; c) failing to provide safe passage between Gaza and the West Bank; d) continuing to confiscate Palestinian lands; and e) failing to release Palestinian prisoners and detainees."[66] As Thomas L. Friedman wrote: "If the Israeli-Palestinian peace process unravels, the entire structure of Arab-Israeli peace since Camp David will be eroded. Egypt, Jordan, Morocco, Qatar, let alone Syria, will never be able to proceed toward real normalization with Israel if they do not have the cover of a real Israeli-Palestinian peace agreement."[67]

To conclude this case study, let me note that perhaps the most important lesson we can draw from it in relation to terrorism—just as we can draw from a study of the root causes of IRA, Basque, or other contemporary examples of political and/or moralistic/religious terrorism—is that these types of terrorism cannot be brought under control, let alone eradicated, even by the harshest counterterrorist methods and measures, if their root causes are not eliminated by peaceful means. But the peaceful elimination of their root causes requires genuine compromise through patient, often lengthy and frustrating negotiations, in which all sides receive as much justice and satisfaction as the practical realities allow.

Notes

1. Quotations in this paragraph are from Leonard B. Weinberg and Paul Davis, *Introduction to Political Terrorism* (New York, 1989), 38-39.

2. Unfortunately it has become quite fashionable, on the part of the authorities and the media in the United States, to label all sorts of acts of murder, kidnapping, bombing, and other unlawful and violent acts "terrorism," in the absence of the kind of knowledge of their actual or possible perpetrators I have described. Such labeling often occurs before any suspects are apprehended or brought to justice, or even before their identity is known. True, the label "terrorism" is sometimes attached to acts of violence directed against the government, as when a government building is bombed, giving the authorities and the media the presumption that the perpetrators are angry at the government. But even that is far from sufficient evidence—given the essential "bifocal" character of terrorism and hence the perpetrators' motives or reasons for their acts—that they are in fact acts of terrorism.

   The tendency of the media to label certain acts of violence terrorism in the absence of supporting evidence is well illustrated by the bombings of the New York City World Trade Center and a United States government building in Oklahoma City. In the former case the bombing was labeled terrorism months before the perpetrators were tried and convicted. In the latter case the label has been applied even though, at the time of this writing, no evidence has been forthcoming as to whether the suspects were the real perpetrators, and whether they were connected with any of the right-wing militia in the country who strongly oppose the government and are prepared to use violence against it.

3. "Kenya," *Collier's Encyclopedia* [New York, 1990] v. 14, 49.

4. A striking example appeared as I was concluding this appendix, in the form of an article by Cal Thomas of the Los Angeles Times, appropriately (albeit not in the sense intended by Thomas) titled "Israel Mustn't Swallow Revisionist History," in the *Milwaukee Journal Sentinel*, 3 July 1966, editorial page. The mixture of fact, fiction, and historical revisionism in the article serves as an excellent illustration of the point I am making.

5. Haig Khatchadourian, "Criteria of Territorial Rights of Peoples and Nations," in *The Territorial Rights of Nations and Peoples*. Studies in World Peace, vol. 2, John R. Jacobson, ed. (Lewiston, NY, 1989), 29-51.

6.   This and the following extract, ibid., 33.

7.   Ibid., 41.

8.   See ibid., 44-45, for an appraisal of that claim.

9.   See e.g., ibid., 47-51.

10. Dan Horowitz, "Diasporas and Communal Conflicts in Divided Societies: The case of Palestine under the British Mandate," in *Modern Diasporas in International Politics*, Gabriel Sheffer, ed. (London, 1986), 301.

11. Philip L. Groisser, *The United States and the Middle East* (Albany, NY, 1982), 117-118.

12. Ibid., 118.

13. Edward Said, *The Question of Palestine* (New York, 1980), 15-16. Italics in original.

14. However, the phrase "foreign group" is too strong since, as noted, there was a continuous Jewish presence in Palestine during the two centuries of the Jewish Diaspora, and since the Jews had been the indigenous inhabitants of part of the land, and Palestinians who inhabited the country at the time of the Arab conquest were, quite possibly, descendants of the Philistines, who lived in parts of it before Abraham.

15. For Arab reactions to the Balfour Declaration, see Anthony Nutting, *The Arabs* (New York, 1964), ch. 25, "The Arabs Betrayed."

16. As described by Adam M. Garfinkle,"Genesis," in *The Arab-Israeli Conflict: Perspectives*, Alvin Z. Rubenstein, ed. (New York, 1984), during the war the British had promised the Sherif of Mecca, Emir Hussein ibn Ali, that the Arabs would be granted political independence if they revolted against the Turks. The deal was made in 1915, "in which Britain recognized and supported the independence of the Arabs in all regions within the limits demanded by the Sherif (namely, the entire Arab rectangle, including Syria, Arabia and Mesopotamia), with the exceptions of portions of Syria lying to the West of the districts of Damascus, Homs, Hama and Aleppo. Depending on the meaning of 'Syria' as a geographical designation, this exception could include Palestine, as the British later held, or it could not, as the Hashemites later argued. . . . The Arab Revolt, led by Hussein's second son, Faisal, and T. E. Lawrence . . . caused the Turks much trouble, and when the dust settled in 1918, Faisal and a ragtag Bedouin army were ensconced in Damascus with British aid." (p. 19)

The French wanted to control the area and were promised as much by the British in the secret Sykes-Picot Agreement. In 1919, although Faisal was able to get the support of the Zionists against the French and a "treaty" of cooperation was agreed upon, the Zionists decided not to oppose the wishes of the British. These included French domination in Damascus "in return for British control of Palestine. Thus, the alliance between Faisal and Weizmann was short-lived." (Garfinkle, "Genesis," 19-20.)

The Sykes-Picot Agreement of 1916 was followed, on 7 November 1918, by another Anglo-French declaration. It stated in part that the objective of France and Britain in fighting in the east the war started by the Germans, was the "complete and definite emancipation of the peoples, governments and administrations deriving their authority from the initiative and free choice of the indigenous populations." (Jukka Nevakivi, *Britain, France and the Arab Middle East, 1914-1920* [London, 1969], app. B, 265.)

Further, in an "Aide-Memoire in regard to the Occupation of Syria, Palestine, and Mesopotamia pending the Decision in regard to Mandates," Article 6 in part states: "The territories occupied by British troops will then be Palestine, defined in accordance with its ancient boundaries," while Article 7 in part reads: "The British government are prepared at any time to discuss the boundaries between Palestine and Syria." (Nevakivi, app. C.)

Finally, in summarizing the situation, Nevakivi, p. 260, comments that the Arab Middle East "was the area where the allied declarations of peace principles and their enactment came into most upsetting conflict. . . . The entente [between Britain and France] resulted in a partition of interests, in the manner of the worst pre-war imperialism" damaging the reputation of both Britain and France in the Arab world. He adds that, in Europe, World War II swept away a great deal of the resentment that arose over the peace-making of France and Britain, but that "it still survives" in the east.

17. Nutting, *The Arabs*, 276; see also 277-278.

18. Ibid., 279.

19. Ibid., 280.

20. Garfinkle, "Genesis," in *The Arab-Israeli Conflict: Perspectives*, Alvin Z. Rubinstein, ed. (New York, 1984), 18. The author significantly adds, p. 19, that Hussein cut a deal with the British in 1915, in which Britain recognized and supported 'the independence of the Arabs in all regions within the limits demanded by the Sherif (namely, the entire Arab rectangle, including Syria, Arabia and Mesopotamia), with the exception of portions of Syria lying to the West of the Districts of Damascus, Homs, Hama and Aleppo." But I cannot see how the author also adds that "depending on the meaning of 'Syria' as a geographical designation, this exception could include Palestine, since Lebanon, not Palestine was (and is) west of the then "districts of Damascus, Homs, Hama and Aleppo." Since biblical times Palestine has always been geographically *south* of these designated districts.

21. The interested reader is referred to Appendix A, "The Anglo-French Agreement of 1916," in Aaron S. Klieman, *Foundations of British Policy in the Arab World: The Cairo Conferences* (Baltimore, 1970), 261-263, and to Nevakivi, appendices B and C (note 16, above).

22. My criticism of British policy, including the Sykes-Picot agreement, on moral grounds, presupposes a view known as political moralism, which maintains (in contrast to political realism or *realpolitik*) that moral assessment is meaningful in and applicable to international relations (see Chapter 4). Traditional just-war theory, appealed to throughout this book, is of course a major application of political moralism.

    In this connection, the following passage by Jukka Nevakivi, *Britain, France, and the Arab Middle East*, 260, is noteworthy: "For the United States government and public opinion the failure of an ideal settlement in Syria seemed to provide a spectacular example of a lack of sincerity among the European allies. According to the evidence given by Robert Lansing [on 20 August 1919], Syria was one of the few cases over which President Wilson threatened to withdraw from the whole settlement and to refuse American membership in the League of Nations."

23. Nutting, *The Arabs*, 332-333.

24. This and the following quotations in this paragraph are from Garfinkle, "Genesis," 22.

25. Ibid., 29.

26. Ibid.

27. Ibid., 31-32.

28. Ibid., 32.

29. Ibid., 36.

30. Ibid., 37.

31. A notorious example well exploited by Israeli propaganda was the irresponsible rhetoric and hyperbole of the first head of the PLO, the pro-Egypt Palestinian attorney Ahmad Shukairy, who boasted that the Arabs would "throw the Jews into the sea." Perhaps no statement by any Arab leader has caused more harm to the Palestinian cause in world opinion than that thoughtless remark, since Shukairy's words were interpreted absolutely literally in the West as well as in Israel.

32. The classic example was of course Jamal Abdel-Nasser's confrontation with Israel, which, together with Jordan's unfortuante involvement, led to the disastrous 1967 Six-Day War and cost the Palestinians the West Bank, the Gaza Strip, and East Jerusalem.

33. Although once it started, it came to enjoy the PLO's blessing and support.

34. With the notable exception of some of the Gulf states, including perhaps most prominently the Saudi ruling elites, the phenomenon is seen in the economic and educational spheres, if not also in the political sphere.

35. Since the Egyptian-Israeli peace treaty, Egypt has become the second greatest recipient of official American largesse.

36. Philip Groisser, *United States and Middle East*, 156.

37. Ibid.

38. Ibid. The parallel with Britain's later decision to seek to establish a national home for the Jews in Palestine is obvious. But although laudable from a humanitarian point of view, nineteenth- and early twentieth-century Americn sympathy for the reestablishment of a homeland for the Jews in Palestine did not seem to show even a passing concern for the rights and welfare of the indigenous Palestinian population at that time.

39. Arab students at the American University of Beirut with whom I used to discuss Middle East politics during the 1950s and 1960s were invariably perplexed about the U.S.'s apparent belief that it was in its self-interest to support Israel, at the cost of antagonizing the hundreds of millions of Arabs and Muslims in the area and the rest of the world, especially given the latters' vastly greater economic, political and strategic importance for the United States.

40. It is not clear whether the Clinton administration countenances, or would countenance, an independent Palestinian state, with east Jerusalem as its capital.

41. *Toward Peace in Palestine*, Hatem I. Hussaini, ed., Arab Information Center (Washington, DC, 1976), 3-18. No date is given for the speech.

42. Hatem I. Hussaini, "Toward a Peaceful Solution of the Palestine Conflict," in *Toward Peace in Palestine*, 44-48.

43. Ibid., 47.

44. All quotations in this paragraph, ibid.

45. Norton Mezvinsky, in *Zionism: The Dream and the Reality*, Gary V. Smith, ed. Quoted in *Toward Peace in Palestine*, 56-57.

46. Another solution, that of a two-state federation was proposed by Noam Chomsky and some other writers. In 1971 Chomsky wrote: "The Jews and the Arabs of the former Palestine claim national rights to the same territory. Each national group demands, with justice, the right

of self-government and cultural autonomy. In principle these demands could be reconciled within a federal framework, perhaps in the form of two federated republics with parity." Chomsky, in *The Arab World. From Nationalism To Revolution*, Abdeen Jabara, ed. Quoted in *Toward Peace in Palestine*, 53.

47. Unfortunately, the Supreme Court of Israel has very recently authorized the use of what was euphemistically called "mild physical and mental pressure" during the interrogation of two suspected Palestinian militants. The "mild pressure"—which independent human rights groups have contemned as torture—included repeated shaking of the suspected militants, who, during the long hours of interrogation are made to sit in a very uncomfortable position with their heads completely covered by a hood. Recently, another Palestinian suspect died in prison, apparently of the "mild pressure."

On November 22 and 23, 1996, the *Milwaukee Journal-Sentinel* reported other documented instances of abuse of Palestinians by Israeli troops. It also reported that to help document future abuse, Yasser Arafat's government "will distribute video cameras to Palestinians living near Israeli checkpoints. . . . The decision was taken after a Palestinian man taped two Israeli border police as they kicked, beat and humiliated six Palestinian laborers caught sneaking into Israel. Two police officers were arrested after the amateur video was broadcast on Israel TV this week."

The report continued, "We want the world to know about this phenomenon. There isn't a single Palestinian who hasn't been abused," Arafat adviser Ahmed Tibi told The Associated Press on Friday.

"The commander of Israel's paramilitary border police said this week that there had been an increase in violence against Palestinians by members of his force, and that 237 complaints had been filed against border police this year."

48. I use quotes around the word "terrorists" because for the most part these are "freedom fighters" resisting Israeli occupation of the so-called security zone in southern Lebanon.

49. *The Price of Peace: The Toll of the Peace Process on Palestinians in the Occupied Territories*, 1 Nov 1991–15 Feb 1992, Jerusalem Media and Communication Centre (East Jerusalem, February 1992).

50. Ibid., 1.

51. Ibid., 15.

52. Ibid., 27-32.

53. Ibid., 17-25.

54. Ibid., 32-37.

55.   As reported by the *Milwaukee Journal-Sentinel* in June 1996, Hamas declared that it will not launch attacks against Israel if Israel stops its "terrorist" attacks against Palestinians. That declaration was not borne out by subsequent events.

56.   Lally Weymouth, "'We Will Not Go Back'," *Newsweek*, 1 July 1996, 43.

57.   Ibid.

58.   "Arab Leaders Warn Netanyahu," *Milwaukee Journal-Sentinel*, 24 June 1996, 1.

59.   Ibid.

60.   Cf. the following, from an editorial in the *Milwaukee Journal-Sentinel* of May 31, 1996, "At best, Natanyahu is a reluctant supporter of the historic negotiations with the Palestine Liberation Organization. Over the long run, the negotiationg process is irreversible, because the two sides have no choice but to come to terms. But with Netanyahu as prime minister, the negotiations could slow, or even stop. Such an outcome could easily provoke new violence, and not only between Israel and Lebanon-based guerillas, but also between Israel and Palestinians who live under Israeli rule. Any bloodletting, particularly if lengthy, could poison Israel's relations with the Arab world. It would almost certainly doom any early agreement with Syria."

61.   "Arab Leaders Warn Netanyahu," 1.

62.   Weymouth, "'We Will Not Go Back'," 43.

63.   Ibid.

64.   Associated Press and New York Times, "Security Council Seeks Halt to Violence in Israel," the *Milwaukee Journal-Sentinel*, 29 September 1996, 4.

65.   Jerome Socolovsky, Associated Press, "Rabin's Grave Symbolizes What 'Could Have Been'," the *Milwaukee Journal-Sentinel*, 29 September 1996.

66.   James M. Barrett, "Middle East Backgrounder," in "The News Behind the News of the U.S. Foreign Policy," the *Milwaukee Journal-Sentinel*, 7 October 1996.

67.   Thomas L. Friedman, "Now I Get to Talk, Bibi, While You Get to Listen," the *Milwaukee Journal-Sentinel*, 4 October 1996.

Glossary of Key Terms

Act-Utilitarianism. "An ethical theory which emphasizes particular actions to be taken in particular situations to bring about the greatest benefit."[1]

Antiterrorism. Judicial measures and strategies employed by governments and private concerns that are designed to combat and prevent terrorism.

Civil disobedience. "A man must honour his duties to his God and to his conscience, and if these conflict with his duty to [obey the laws of] the State, then he is entitled, in the end, to do what he judges to be right. If he decides that he must break the law,. . . then he must submit to the judgment and punishment that the State imposes."[2]

Competent authority. In just war theory, the rule that war must be waged by a "competent authority," such as a government.

Counterterrorism. "Measures emphasizing the tactical force option, for prevention, preemption, or retaliation against terrorist acts."[3]

Deontological ethics. "The view that emphasizes the performance of duty, rather than results, as the sign of right action."[4]

Essentialist concepts. A concept "Y" is an essentialist concept if all the things that are called "Ys" are so called because they have a quality or a set of qualities in common, by virtue of which they are all called "Ys." Cf. family resemblance concepts.

Family resemblance concepts. A concept "X" is a family resemblance concept if the things it refers to "instead of having defining characteristics common to all "Xs"—the things it refers to—"we see a complicated network of similarities overlapping and criss-crossing: sometimes over-all similarities, sometimes similarities of detail." Cf. essentialist concepts.[5]

"Freedom fighting". As distinguished from terrorism, the use of force or violence in pursuit of freedom. In a broad sense, freedom fighting includes uprising, rebellion and revolution, civil war and defensive war or guerrilla warfare, in puruit of national liberation against an oppressive domestic ruler, government, or regime.

Genocide. The extermination or attempted extermination of a people planned or carried out by a state.

Human rights. Also called "natural rights." Very strong moral entitlements, defenses, and protections or "protective norms," that human beings have not in any particular capacity or by virtue of some particular transaction or relationship (special rights) but simply as human beings.

Just war theory. A theory, going back to the Middle Ages, detailing the moral conditions for a "just" or morally right war.

Jus in bello. In just war theory, "rules that determine *how* a war should be fought once it has begun."

Jus ad bellum. In just war theory, "rules that determine *when* it is permissible or obligatory to begin a war."[7]

Just cause. "The most important of the *jus ad bellum* rules is the rule that the moral use of military force requires a just cause." That is, "For the sake of peace" (Aristotle), for "wrong received" (Cicero), or for "self-defense as a response to aggression" (United Nations), "are among the various historical views of just cause."[8]

Just peace. In modern just war theory, the rule that "for war to be just, the winning side must not only have obtained justice for itself: it must not have achieved it at the price of violating the rights of others. A just war must lead to a just peace."[9]

Moralistic/religious terrorism. Terrorist acts that aim at some putative ultimate or long-range moral/religious objective, such as overthrow of an oppressive ruler or regime, or legitimate territorial gain.

Necessity. In just war theory, the principle that "everything permissible [in war] must be necessary": "that *wanton* destruction is forbidden."[10]

Open-textured concepts. Non-sharply defined or demarcated concepts, involving borderline or marginal indeterminacy (Max Black); concepts that have an "open texture," that lack boundaries in all directions (Friedrich Waismann). Opposite: "closed" concepts.

Political terrorism. Terrorist acts directed at governments and their agents or agencies, motivated by a long-range or ultimate political goal, such as national liberation, the regaining of territory occupied by the target government, or other political ends.

Predatory terrorism. Terrorist acts motivated by greed.

Principle (or doctrine) of double effect. A Catholic doctrine or principle which, in one main version, maintains that an act which has a "double effect," i.e., produces both good and bad consequences, is morally right or permissible if the good effects exceed the bad effects, the agent's intent is to bring about the good effects, and the good effects are independent of and not a consequence of the bad effects.

Principle of discrimination or noncombatant immunity. In just war theory, the principle that "civilian life and property should not be subjected to military force: military force must be directed only at military objectives."[11]

Principle of proportionality. In just war theory, the principle that "the amount of harm that it is morally permissible to produce in pursuit of a just cause should be a function of the moral importance of the cause."[12] This is the *political* principle in *jus ad bellum*. Corresponding to this is the *military* principle of proportionality in *jus in bello*, which states that "the amount of destruction permitted in pursuit of a military objective must be proportionate to the importance of the objective."[13]

Principle of utility. "We are obligated to act so as to promote the greatest balance of good over evil."[14]

Quasi-essentialist concepts. A concept "S" is a quasi-essentialist concept if like essentialist concepts, all "Ss" have a common defining characteristic, but additionally have a set of crisscrossing similarities of various degrees of specificity or generality, like family resemblance concepts.

Retaliatory terrorism. Terrorist acts motivated by a desire for revenge against a government or agency, or against a particular individual or group for acts of counterterrorism perpetrated against the terrorist or terrorist organization, or his or their compatriots.

Right intention. In traditional just war theory, the rule that "a just war [must] be a war for the right, fought for the sake of the right." For one modern author (Lackey) "the desire for what is morally right [must] be at least *one* of [the] motives" of political leaders, hence that "political leaders must be able to justify their decisions on moral grounds."[15]

Rule-utilitarianism. "An ethical theory which emphasizes rules to be followed in a situation to bring about the greatest benefit."[16]

State terrorism. Terrorism perpetrated by a state against its own citizens or a segment of its citizens, or sponsored by it against another state or government. See terrorism from above.

Terror. As distingushed from terrorism, acts of wanton violence or cruelty that strike terror in the hearts of the populace.

Terrorism. Acts of violence, distinguished from other uses of violence by their "bifocal" character: by the perpetrators' use of often wanton acts of kidnapping, hostage-taking, murder, and the like, against individuals, groups, or institutions (the "immediate victims"), as a means of forcing, e.g., some country, government, or power ("the victimized"), to accede to their economic, political, moralistic or religious demands.

Terrorism from above. Acts of terrorism "perpetrated by governments using their own military or police forces upon their citizens."[17] *See also* state terrorism.

Terrorism from below. Acts of terrorism perpetrated by individuals or groups with a view to destabilizing a government, or to some other political or moralistic/religious end. Especially in time of war, terrorism may be part of a national liberation movement.

Utilitarianism. In classical utilitarianism, such as in Jeremy Bentham and John Stuart Mill, "The ethical doctrine that an action is right if, and only if, it promotes the greatest happiness for the greatest number of people."[18]

Violence. Unlawful use of force.

War. "the controlled use of force ["for political purposes"], undertaken by persons organized in a functioning chain of command."[19]

Notes

1   *Questions that Matter*, Ed. L. Miller, ed. (New York, 1993), 448.

2   Ronald Dworkin, *Taking Rights Seriously* (Cambridge, MA, 1977), 186-187.

3   H. J. Vetter et al., *Perspectives on Terrorism* (Pacific Grove, CA, 1990), 247.

4   Miller, *Questions*, 452.

5   Ludwig Wittgenstein, *Philosophical Investigations* (Oxford, 1963), 32e.

6   Douglas Lackey, *The Ethics of War and Peace* (Englewood Cliffs, NJ, 1989), 29.

7   Ibid.

8   Ibid., 33ff.

9   Ibid., 43.

10   Ibid., 59.

11   Ibid.

12   Ibid.

13   Ibid.

14   Miller, *Questions*, 470.

15   Lackey, *Ethics*, 31f.

16   *Questions that Matter*, 465.

17   Vetter et al., *Perspectives*, 257.

18   Miller, *Questions*, 470.

19   Lackey, *Ethics*, 30.

Index

CONFLICT AND CONSCIOUSNESS
Studies in War, Peace, and Social Thought

Charles P. Webel, General Editor

Human perceptions of and responses to conventional warfare and nuclear weapons are changing. To explore these changes in attitudes and behaviors and to address effectively the issues of war and peace in our time, educators and students, everyday citizens and decision-makers alike must become better informed about the nature and functions of human conflicts and their social, psychological, political, and ideological roots.

CONFLICT AND CONSCIOUSNESS: STUDIES IN WAR, PEACE AND SOCIAL THOUGHT is designed to facilitate this educational process. The principal aim of this series is to illuminate the often-opaque connections that link individual consciousness, personal and collective belief systems, and social practices involving coercion and violence. Since the reasons for wars and the prospects for an enduring peace transcend conventional academic disciplinary boundaries, this series will include cross-disciplinary and unorthodox approaches, as well as more traditional philosophical, social-scientific, and humanistic monographs.

For further information about this series and for the submission of manuscripts, contact:

Professor Charles P. Webel
Saybrook Institute
Graduate School and Research Institute
450 Pacific Street, 3rd floor
San Francisco, CA 94133
e-mail: cwebel@igc.apc.org
fax: 415-433-9271